PSYCHOEVALUATION:

ADAPTATION-Distribution-adjustment

Milton E. Hahn
Professor of Psychology
The University of California
Los Angeles

McGraw-Hill Book Company, Inc.
New York, San Francisco, Toronto, London

PSYCHOEVALUATION: ADAPTATION-Distribution-adjustment

Library of Congress Catalog Card Number 62-19761

25509

Dedicated to
the memory of
Donald H. Dabelstein
Federal Office
of Vocational Rehabilitation
and
Donald G. Paterson
Professor of Psychology
University of Minnesota

Two normal, mature, self-actualizing individuals
who gave richly of themselves for the good of so many.

Preface

Psychoevaluation is a book with heroes and heroines: the normal, mature, self-actualizing men and women who have provided the solid foundations on which Western civilization has been built. These *uncommon* men and women comprise a minority group which suffers many of the ills which beset minorities. They are too few in numbers to be highly regarded in political councils, although their organizations and personal stature provide some balance. Economically they are targets because their combined earnings and possessions provide a tax source far richer and more essential than that of "the malefactors of great wealth" about whom so much is said in alternate Novembers. Socially they suffer because of their middle-class virtues of thrift, integrity, and the compulsion not to waste time.

And yet, to this group we have assigned the responsibility for those things we hold most precious. Our biological survival we assign to those in the medical profession. Our liberties, property, and some of the pursuit of happiness are in trust to the lawyers and the courts. Our jobs, careers, and scale of living fall heavily to those who provide leadership in business and industry. These uncommon men and women have written our novels and our poetry, our textbooks and dictionaries, and our state and national constitutions. They have composed and performed our best music, painted our pictures and sculptured our ornaments and statues, created our inventions, and mothered and fathered our on-coming generations of self-actualizers. They are found in our classrooms and laboratories; they have led us in war and in peace; and where statesmanship has emerged from politics, they have been present. In our religious convictions and practices, they are the leaders. Philosophers, historians, and philanthropists in their time are numbered among them. It seems appropriate, then, that in a century of the common man at least one day (and one book) should be devoted to them.

From the standpoint of personality and learning theory, the approach is eclectic. Acknowledgment is made particularly to the influence of Gordon Allport for his emphasis on the unique qualities of the individual personality, Raymond Cattell for his contributions to theory, method, and cutting through the semantic mazes, and Gardner Murphy for his broad biosocial formulations which permit so much room for speculation and hypothesizing. Terman and Oden have provided research findings which in many ways have shaped the materials in this book. John Darley, John Holland, Theda Hagenah, and Donald Super, among others, have provided important directions regarding motivation in their contributions to the field of measured interests. Some readers will remark on the congruence of much that follows with sensitivity training. Because this book is aimed at the individual and his relations with a single professional psychologist, little reference will be found to the important contributions of sensitivity training with its group applications and implications.

The title of the book and a process, *Psychoevaluation,* was coined to do the work which no other word in common usage appears to do. Therapy seemed inappropriate for obvious reasons. The word is used to mean one-to-one professional relations between a *client* and a psychologist, with the client in control of process content and the psychologist providing flexible process structure. Psychoevaluation is not just an extension of either counseling or psychotherapy. It is not a process which holds great promise for the solid, invaluable, average man or woman who "needs help." It is not a tight practice which lends itself easily to the machinations of the graduate curriculum makers. It is not a new way of describing the giving of advice. It is not aimed at curing anything or changing the personality structure of the individual or the world. It is not a new speciality which requires the organization of a division in the American Psychological Association.

Psychoevaluation is based on the knowledge and skills which have been the groundwork of counseling and psychotherapy—assessment, diagnosis, evaluation, and communication. It is aimed at a small, but exceedingly important, segment of the population described as *normal, mature,* and *self-actualizing*—those who will save time and some anxiety by better insight into the three dynamics. The present practitioners arrived at this status by self-education and experience integrated with the knowledge and insights which came from "pure" psychology. The *with* client-psychologist relation, in which the client, not the psychologist, controls much of the process, distinguishes it from practice in which there is a heavier loading of *to* and *for*. The majority of those who work with the normal, mature, self-actualizing individual are recruited from the psychologists immersed in problem patterns of ADAPTATION-Distribution-adjustment.

Although the English and English *A Comprehensive Dictionary of Psychological and Psychoanalytical Terms* is used as a standard reference, some uncommon usages will be encountered. In Chapter 1 the reader will discover "degrees-of-choice-freedom," "becoming," "being," "having been," "reaping," and "sowing." The semantically debased "counseling," "clinical," and "industrial" are avoided in favor of the awkward, but more descriptive, "ADAPTATION-Distribution-adjustment," "ADJUSTMENT-Adaptation-distribution," in referring to professional psychologists and their operations. The intention of this usage is to indicate the loadings of competencies and interests judged to be most characteristic of the professional effort. "Self-actualization" is in line with Maslow and with English and English rather than the organismic, single growth-principle concept of motivation.

Catastrophic happenings do change the course of events. The Los Angeles fire, in November, 1961, destroyed some 250 pages of appendixes and the bibliography cards upon which they, and that section of the manuscript, depended. It is understandable why the writer saved a copy of Maslow's *Motivation and Personality,* but it is not quite so clear why he walked past more than four hundred laboriously prepared bibliography cards and the manuscript for the appendixes. The result is that the recovered portion of the previously intended book is published here, and the appendixes are being reconstructed for future publication. The appendixes would have made the materials much more appropriate as a supplement to graduate training in professional psychology or as a possible text.

Milton E. Hahn

Acknowledgments

No book is completed without the help of many others. To my wife, Margaret, I am most indebted. Her patience, her willingness to share drudgery, and her skillful diagnosis and treatment of *taedium vitae* and *cacoethes scribendi,* are responsible for whatever success is forthcoming. Malcolm MacLean provided rich discussion in the planning stages of this book and applied his editorial lancet to some of the chapters.

Lois Langland, Charles Titus, and Robert Waldrop read the rough draft of the manuscript, and their suggestions and criticisms were most helpful. Arthur Waites, William Levy, and Robert Hadley gave critical attention to some of the chapters. Bruce Rolf, M.D., provided views from a nonpsychologist standpoint. On specific points George Lehner offered much insight.

To the students in my seminars who gave concepts a very rough time, a particularly hearty thanks. I am very grateful as well to Mrs. Sharon Whitehouse who typed the manuscript, edited and excised embryonic *errata,* helping to produce the final product.

Because others so frequently say so much better what one wants to say, flavor is lost if the original statements cannot be presented. Appreciation and gratitude are given to the publishers below for their generous permission to quote.

The American Psychological Association
Harcourt, Brace & World, Inc.
Harper & Row
Holt, Rinehart and Winston, Inc.
McGraw-Hill Publishing Company, Inc.
David McKay Company, Inc.
Prentice-Hall, Inc.
W. B. Saunders Company
Stanford University Press
The University of Chicago Press
The University of Michigan Press
The University of Wisconsin Press
John Wiley & Sons, Inc.

Table of Contents

Chapter 1

PSYCHOEVALUATION

Consideration of uncommon men and women as heroes and heroines forces consideration of uncommon methodologies. This does not imply the need for inventing immediately new and startling approaches to the study and understanding of human behavior. The professional psychologist, using the foundations supplied by his researching brethren, has been ingenious in exploring and manipulating the personality dimensions of those he serves—clients or patients. In the realm of human *adjustment* problems, the workings of numerous social forces including war and urbanization have filled our libraries with materials about mental illness, its cure or amelioration, and its prevention. There have been times when we have been certain that all solutions to man's problems lay in adjusting him.

In large part because of the socioeconomic complexities of the Western cultures, the problems of social and self-distribution to jobs, careers, formal education, the military, business, industry, and government have received much of some professional psychologists' attention beginning with the World War I era. We have passed through periods when all our problems appeared solvable if we tested-factored, assessed-distributed everyone.

Although the literature of professional psychology pays homage to working *with* people, most of us who have come through the periods of distributing or adjusting others have been, for the most part, doing something *to* and *for* our clients and patients. There is some evidence that the century of the common man is devoted in large part to doing things *to* and *for* others. Emphasis in this book is placed on *working with clients,* who, being normal, mature, and self-actualizing, will seldom willingly permit a psychologist or anyone else to do things *to* them, or even *for* them.

As is so frequently the case, someone else has said what we would like to say better than we can say it. In this instance it is J. Huxley (1960, 20–21) to whom we turn.

Though natural selection is an ordering principle, it operates blindly; it pushes life onwards from behind, and brings about improvement automatically, without conscious purpose or any awareness of an aim. Psycho-social selection too acts as an ordering principle. But it pulls man onwards from in front. For it always involves some awareness of an aim, some element of true purpose. Throughout biological evolution the selective mechanism remained essentially unchanged. But in psycho-social evolution the selective mechanism itself evolves as well as its products. It is a goal-selecting mechanism, and the goals that it selects will change with the picture of the world and of human nature provided by man's increasing knowledge. Thus as human comprehension, knowledge and understanding increase, the aims of evolving man can become more clearly defined, his purpose more conscious and more embracing.

In the light of our present knowledge man's most comprehensive aim is seen not as mere survival, not as numerical increase, not as increased complexity of organization or increased control over his environment, but as greater fulfilment—the fuller realization of more possibilities by the human species collectively and more of its component members individually. . . . Once greater fulfilment is recognized as man's ultimate or dominant aim, we shall need a science of human possibilities to help guide the long course of psycho-social evolution that lies ahead.

In this book the major concern is with Huxley's science of human possibilities with emphasis on individuals and their adaptations and distributions. One hesitates to coin words and to change standard meanings of words in common usage. Although the attempt is made to avoid either undesirable alternative, both crimes will be found at the misdemeanor level. The coined word is *psychoevaluation.* The reader will find different usages of words in such terms as *degrees-of-choice-freedom* in reference to alternatives of behavior among and between which the individual is deemed to have the power of final decision. Although it may border on the pedantic, definitions will be offered from standard sources for many of the concepts used. We begin with a definition of psychoevaluation which is not found in a standard source.

Psychoevaluation is a process of making appropriate and relevant knowledges and skills of the psychologist available to individuals who are normal, mature, and self-actualizing. Its major emphasis is on human problems of *adaptation* and *distribution* with clients who are evaluated as competent adequately to deal with their internalized problems of *adjustment.* It emphasizes a client-psychologist relationship pattern of WITH-For-to, in which *to* is the end of the relationship continuum where control is almost completely the psychologist's, and *with* the end which indicates almost complete client control.

Psychoevaluation relies on the processes of *assessment* and *evaluation* of personality dimensions as foundations for structuring its applications. It goes beyond assessment in terms of the type of client, the much longer usefulness of outcomes, and the complexity and number of personality dimensions and factors dealt with. Psychoevaluation differs from evaluation in that it carries fewer implications of *to* and *for* and avoids the narrow synonym for evaluation, *educational measurement.* Although psychoevaluation deals with the personality dimension relationships against standards, the standards are usually less specific and the objectives of the process more long-circuited than is true of evaluation. Psychoevaluation affords structure to client self-study in the interest of long-range client life planning, usually for the last three or four decades of life expectancy.

Inasmuch as the remainder of the book is about the process of psychoevaluation, its clients, and practitioners, this chapter will be devoted to a discussion of terms and philosophy and a preview of the chapters which follow. Here, in the interests of clarification, two negatives are emphasized before becoming positive.

Psychoevaluation is not synonymous with counseling or counseling psychology. Counseling as a process has become a badly eroded term. Many words are saved here if the reader will consult English and English, *A Comprehensive Dictionary of Psychological and Psychoanalytical Terms* (1958). Their definition supports the generalization-to-meaninglessness hypothesis. There is "counseling" for problems involving marriage, the law, vocations, avocations, guidance, dormitory life, recreation, youth camps, groups, individuals, religion, education, sex, and a greater number of other problems not listed here. The title has no legal protection, requires no professional training, and unless defined by several words used with it, has no meaning.

Counseling psychology has established itself at the professional level and is protected as a professional title through the ABEPP diploma and the certification and licensing laws for professional psychologists in a number of states. In the APA structure it is one of the present three largest divisions. However, although many counseling psychologists are qualified to work with the majority of clients, there has been a tendency to relate practice to formal educational settings, assessment, and a client age range of from fifteen to thirty years. In general, members of this group have avoided private practice. The research and writings of counseling psychologists show little emphasis on the normal, mature, self-actualizing individual. There are fine contributions to clients in the decades of *becoming,* but the contributions to clients in the sowing and reaping periods of *being* and in the period of *having been* have been for the most part left to others.

Psychoevaluation is not closely related to the objectives and methods of psychotherapy. The adequately trained professional psychologist, even though devoted to major practice with *client,* not *patient,* problems, should be competent to diagnose mental illness or disturbance which requires psychotherapy. However, this does not imply either interest or competence in treating mental illness, restructuring personality, or employment in a medical setting. In psychoevaluation there is no attempt to cure anyone or to make marked changes in behavior. Psychotherapists are "talking" not "working" doctors, and the interview is the chief vehicle for therapy. The reader will find a more detailed discussion of distinctions between psychotherapists and nonpsychotherapists in Chapters 8 and 9 so that there is little need to belabor the point here. The nonpsychotherapist does, however, have a more flexible communication armamentarium than major reliance on the interview (Chapter 7). As was indicated in the preface, buttressed by scattered but impressive evidence in the research literature, there appear to be personality differences which make one psychologist happy with patients and another with clients. "Rockheads" tend to be nonpsychotherapists; "bleeding hearts," psychotherapists.

PSYCHOEVALUATION

To meet the problems of reader-author communication, it seems desirable to clear away a bit of semantic brush at this point. As has been stated above, the process under discussion is not perceived as identical with any of the present areas of practice in which ABEPP grants diplomas. Therefore, to avoid confusion, word usage requires some attention. The reader will find the word *communication* used instead of "interview" in many places where he is accustomed to the latter. Communication is used to indicate any interchange of ideas, feeling, or information between a client and a psychologist in a professional setting. Although the interview is specified as a method of communication, *bibliocommunication, nonverbal communication, personal documents, records, recordings,* and *recording transcriptions* will also be encountered when there is specific reference to them and when they are considered as the most appropriate method of communication. Chapter 7 deals specifically with these matters.

Adaptation and *adjustment* are at times encountered in the literature used as synonyms. Here they are treated as interacting, but discrete, processes. Adaptation has an aura of biological survival, to which we have gradually added implications of psychological survival. Beginning with Olds (1958, 237), authority is invoked.

> By adaptive behavior we mean some change which makes the organism more fitted for survival in a given environment. The change may be a rigidly determined, automatic response to a need, as when energy demands are met by an increase in blood pressure, or oxygen demands by an increase in respiratory movement. The change may, however, be less rigid, as when the demands of a new environment are met by alteration in behavior repertory. In both cases the main causal antecedent of the change is a motivational requirement, and the outcome is a better adjustment of the animal to its environment.

Cattell (1957, 568) agrees with Olds when he says:

> *Adaptation* is used in the basic biological and social sense that an individual is well adapted when he and a community of persons with similar habits have a higher than average survival rate. It does not ask by what internal conflict or lack of conflict the individual is able to produce these well-adapted responses, but is simply an index of how sociobiologically effective the behavior is. Insanity, for example, is generally highly maladaptive, but a neurotic could be well adapted at the cost of unhappiness and conflict.

Cattell emphasizes nuances which will be reinforced in these pages. Adaptation has connotations of externalization. In social environments there is more than a trace of the "minimum essentials of conformity" to group mores. We interpret the "higher than average survival rate" of Cattell to mean psychological as well as biological survival. Because these and other related considerations will be dealt with at greater length in Chapters 2 and 3, our point is made here sufficiently by the above.

Adjustment, as we will use it, is internalized and refers, in the main, to the intradynamics of the individual. Personal feelings, emotions, and perceptions make adjustment judgments more a matter of clinical inference than is true of adaptation. Again quoting Cattell (1957, 568):

Adjustment describes the goodness of the internal arrangements by which an adaptation is maintained. Goodness of adjustment is the obverse of conflict and would be synonymous with happiness if *conscious* freedom from internal friction were alone concerned, but adjustment means freedom from pressures, conflicts, and repressions, insofar as possible, throughout *the whole dynamic structure.* There should be some tendency for adjustment and adaptation to be positively correlated, but in principle it is possible for a person to be perfectly adjusted, e.g., with some happy delusion, but quite maladapted, or perfectly adapted, e.g., a successful spy in a foreign country, at the cost of great internal tensions and conflicts.

More homely negative relationships between adaptation and adjustment are illustrated by eyeglasses, porcelain dentures, and toupees. Again, a more detailed consideration of adjustment will be found in another chapter.

Distribution is the third word in our adaptation-adjustment-distribution pattern trilogy for practice in professional psychology. Distribution is used both to indicate distribution by a social agency, such as government, private enterprise, and the military, wherein the individual is assigned his position and status, and in *self-distribution* where self-actualization is primary. In terms of professional practice in psychology, the following loadings may be substituted to some extent for clinical, industrial, and counseling psychology.

ADJUSTMENT-Adaptation-distribution
DISTRIBUTION-Adaptation-adjustment
ADAPTATION-DISTRIBUTION-Adjustment

Psychoevaluation has a pattern of its own: ADAPTATION-Distribution-adjustment. The chief reason for emphasis on the labels in our trilogy of function is to avoid the affective loadings with which *clinical, counseling,* and, to a lesser extent, *industrial* psychology have become weighted.

Assessment will be used to designate an important subprocess within psychoevaluation. An expanded discussion of the term will be found in Chapter 9. In limiting its meaning we wish it to express the evaluation of the relative statics of personality, e.g., trait-like patterns of behavior which are relatively consistent in the life-style of the individual over a long span of years. Further, we tend to assess against criteria for a quite specific purpose. Thus, psychographs of individuals are prepared for comparison with norm groups for purposes of employment, school admission, horizontal or vertical movement in an industrial situation, or to diagnose conditions affecting or affected by health. Assessment is a procedure or process which usually undertakes to do something to or for the individual. It appears to contribute most when problems of distribution are involved, although it has some uses in the area of adjustment. The writings of Hull (1928), Bingham (1937), Super (1949), Super and Crites (1962), and Cottle and Downie (1960) are excellent examples of assessment philosophy and methodology.

THE OBJECTIVES OF PSYCHOEVALUATION

In considering psychoevaluation as a process within the province of professional psychology, it is necessary in describing and defining it that the objectives be stated as clearly as possible. These objectives are very close to those stated by the conference on the training of psychological counselors at the University of Michigan in 1949 and 1950 (Bordin, 1950). As stated in this conference report, the consensus objectives were:

1. Increasing the accuracy of the individual's self-percept.
2. Increasing the accuracy of the individual's environmental perceptions.
3. Integrating the individual's self-percepts and his environmental perceptions.

4. Presenting relevant information.
5. Improving the individual's planning and execution.

Although the deliberations of the conference also were concerned with problems of adjustment, the statements above appear to be chiefly concerned with adaptation. The author adds to the conference consensus objectives one which is chiefly a matter of adjustment:

6. Increasing the individual's ability to gain, and enjoy, personal satisfactions and happiness.

Three dynamics are extracted from these objectives. The *first* dynamic is the intraindividual personality structure. It is involved in "increasing the accuracy of the individual's self-percept" as well as in the psychologist's understanding of a client or patient. It is to this area that much of our formal course work in psychology is devoted, both undergraduate and graduate. We might call it the "psychotherapeutic" dynamic. The *second* dynamic is the not-self dynamic—surrounds, situations, fields, and environment. It is interthings and interpeople. In terms of professional training for psychologists, it tends to be much less attended to in formal course offerings. Adequate practica and internships provide much of our training background in this regard. Too often practica and internships involve very narrow exposures, such as hospital or formal educational settings. The *third* dynamic is the interaction dynamic. It can be expressed as $3 = 1 + 2$. If 1 or 2 is missing, or weak, 3 has difficulty.

The conference deliberations indicated the growing attention in psychology to perception and reality testing. A balance was maintained between ideographic and nomothetic viewpoints. In modifying and extending the objectives for psychologists to develop a process with a different clientele and patterning of purpose, this attention to perception, reality testing, and ideographic-nomothetic balance will be followed. The differences between and among objectives for counseling psychology and psychoevaluation are a result of the chronological, psychological, and sociological maturity of clients in the age range from thirty upwards.

Client Self-perception and Understanding —the First Dynamic

Mature people know much about themselves. In fact, they know more about themselves than others can ever know. Despite this, one of the major reasons why the psychologist, psychiatrist, and related professional workers are useful to them in our culture is that the layman frequently does not have an adequate concept and construct structure within which to view his self-images in appropriate focus. The essential service which the psychologist performs is to present structure cognitively in an affective matrix.

In later chapters specific consideration will be given to hypotheses and theories on which this chapter is based. In dealing with perception, for example, the writing and researches of psychologists such as F. H. Allport (1955) and Solley and Murphy (1960) will be in evidence. Here we deal with process in broad strokes, leaving the details for more intensive consideration along the way. Our generalizations concerning self-perception and understanding are just that at this point—descriptive generalizations for the purpose of setting a stage.

Self-understanding is possible for the individual only within the framework of the static and dynamic perceptions which are at his disposal. If psychologists cannot formulate generally accepted theories concerning learning, thinking, personality development, and organization, with a reasonably precise specialized vocabulary based on years of training and experience in professional communication, we cannot always expect the psychological layman to accomplish these formulations for himself. Systematic, valid, parsimonious, and integrated self-images are possible, but often more difficult for persons without professional aid.

If the relative statics of assessment can be used as a foundation for client-psychologist communication, without damaging concept dilution through nontechnical language, the entry to client understanding of the more complex intrapersonal dynamics is often easier. Within the perceptual and experiential limitations of the client, a clearer self-image may be developed.

Client Perception and Understanding of Environment —the Second Dynamic

We have, in the past, attended so closely to the important considerations of intrapersonal dynamics and statics that we have paid too little attention to environmental dynamics—the cultures and subcultures in which we are immersed. Sociology has been more concerned with social-environmental dynamics, perhaps reversing the psychologist's emphasis by neglecting intrapersonal dynamics.

Social and industrial psychologists appear to have emphasized cultural dynamics and developed a greater familiarity with their dimensions than have the psychologists who have concentrated on the adaptation and adjustment problems of individual patients or clients. And yet, professional psychologists who serve mature, normal clients should be as familiar, or almost as familiar, with a mass of relevant data concerned with societal and cultural dynamics as with those of the individual. The tasks of promoting more valid reality testing with clients would be far easier if we could deal with client perception directly. However, in studying perception of any kind at present, we can deal only with inferences drawn from behaviors—expressive movements, life-styles, and verbal responses.

In dealing with social environment, the psychologist must be sensitive to the tendency of individuals to carry with them, like a turtle his shell, a subcultural half generation. If it is true that the neural nets and circuits of the cerebral cortex, which provide our situational frames and points of reference for goal-directed behavior, have been given their broad but quite rigid form by age twenty, perception and behavior must be understood in terms of cultural and subcultural values, sentiments, goals, and other dimensions of the temporal environment in which the client has been moving from birth to age twenty. Our economic competition and social participation tend to be with those not more than ten years younger or older than ourselves. It seems reasonable that, holding our relative status symbols, roles, and masks in this half generation of time, we do not perceive consensus reality identically with those ten years ahead of, or behind, us chronologically.

Crisis stamping is of importance in this regard. Clients in the age group we are considering may have experienced World War I, the Depression of the 1930s, World War II, and the cold war. In perceiving today's events it will make a difference in client perception if he was five, fifteen, twenty, or forty years of age at the crisis periods. Marital status, familial and financial responsibilities, religion, and geographical location are other important aspects of crisis periods which affect values, goals, and motivations. It is not necessary to belabor the point that few psychologists will claim great competence in the area of broad cultural dynamics.

Adequate Integration and Interaction of Self- and Environmental Perception and Understanding—the Third Dynamic

Gordon Allport (1937, 213–231) provides an excellent door through which to enter consideration of the individual who has achieved self- and environmental adaptation and adjustment. In defining and describing what he considered to be three crucial dimensions in the mature self, he says (213–214):

> In the first place, the developed person is one who has a variety of autonomous interests: that is, he can lose himself in work, in contemplation, in recreation, and in loyalty to others.
> He participates with warmth and vigor in whatever pursuits have for him acquired value. Egocentricity is not the mark of the mature personality. . . .
>
> The second requirement is a curiously subtle factor complementing the first. We may call it *self-objectification,* that peculiar detachment of the mature person when he surveys his own pretensions in relation to his abilities, his present objectives in relation to possible objectives for himself, his own equipment in comparison with the equipment of others, and his opinion of himself in relation to the opinion others hold of him. This capacity for self-objectification is *insight,* and it is bound in subtle ways with the *sense of humor.* . . .
>
> Since there is an obvious antithesis between the capacity for losing oneself in vigorous participation and the capacity for standing off, contemplating oneself, perhaps with amusement, a third integrative, factor

is required in the mature personality, namely, *a unifying philosophy of life*. Such a philosophy is not necessarily articulate, at least not always articulate in words.

Few of us demonstrate an exceptionally high level of achievement relative to all three of these criteria. But the goal of many of us is to approach them. The psychologist who deals professionally with chronologically mature, normal clients seldom can hope that he will lead the client to achieving such maturity, nor is this a primary goal. If individuals understand the words for the structure of concepts and can conceptualize the substance of Allport's meaning, we can hope that movement may take place where some client steps are self-taken toward a greater maturity. If we believe that thinking takes place in situational frames of reference, and if new structures for organizing the data of thinking are provided (and cognitively and affectively accepted), covert, and at times overt, changes in behavior may occur.

The learning processes, particularly those at the symbolic levels, are important if men and women are to change self-images and cultural perceptions. Client perceptions may enlarge or contract, change focus, and take new forms as maturity shifts the value systems under the impact of goal orientation and motivational changes. It is possible that for some clients, the psychologist may provide systematic directional structures which will facilitate better perceptions for this client learning. He at least may hope that ultimate, and sometimes inevitable, conclusions will have a personal impact more rapidly and with less pain.

Discussion in detail of the concepts above will be encountered later in this book in the sections devoted to personality structure and learning. Self-actualization for individuals may be a smoother path if there is some psychologist-provided map in the form of organized concept structuring as crude pointers of direction and alternative roads to more satisfying personal integration.

Personal Satisfactions and Happiness

Departure is made here from the conference objectives cited earlier in this chapter. The viewpoint taken in this book regarding anxieties is that they are, within normal ranges, essential for reality testing and perceptual feedback. Personal satisfactions and happiness are also considered essential as partial counterbalances to anxieties. Although there has always been a group of psychologists who refused to exclude emotions and feelings from learning theory, it is heartening in this context to have Mowrer's recent books as reinforcement (1960, 126–211; 1960*a*, 7–8). We also find the reports of Harlow (1954, 170–185) supporting Mowrer's position on some points. There are, of course, critics of these viewpoints, for example Amsel (1961). But the normal, mature client tests his realities and receives feedback from his behaviors. He is beset with lack of assurance, lack of information, and lack of skills in meeting the environmental situations of social living in our culture (see Chapter 7). Comparable to a young man or woman making an educational or vocational choice, our older client will seek consensus confirmation of his intentions (Hahn and MacLean, 1955, 40–62).

Unless the results of a voluntary exposure to professional communication with a psychologist were hope, anticipation, and closure, there would be little point in making use of the skills of our psychologists. We do not consider these emotional components as direct outcomes of psychoevaluation. We do consider them, however, as results of self-understanding, understanding of the environment, and a satisfactory and realistic integration of these understandings. Maturity should yield a fair balance of reward through long-circuited planning.

Saving of Client Time

In the work of the counseling psychologist with college and university students, the time-saving element is very clear. Realistic student choices of curricula and professional objectives can be shown, in some instances, to save the client one or more years of time and the college appreciable amounts of staff time. With the mature client this time-saving is not so easily or clearly demonstrable. One example should suffice to indicate the general direction of our thinking about this consideration. Some therapists believe that their professional practices "can do no harm." While there are undoubtedly instances where this is true, it violates the goal with which we are concerned. If a "not harmful," but also "not helpful" process consumes a month or more of time before the client or the practitioner discovers that it is not helpful and arranges for experiences that are helpful, damage may occur from the loss of time. Certainly there must be some connection between the not harmful treatment and the damage from time lapse? In wrongly diagnosed cancer there is little question of probable harm. The wrongly assessed or diagnosed anxiety or psychosis is less spectacular in harmful outcome, but the analogy has some point.

When clients in the last decade of being, or the first decade of having been, have anxieties about slowing down, shifting horizontally to less demanding duties and responsibilities, retirement, or just sheer boredom, lost motion and time may appear serious rather than just irritating. If saving of client time is one of the reasons the client came to the psychologist, one must assume also that this objective has some importance for the practitioner. In addition, professional services are a scarce and expensive commodity. When our psychologist makes more than his share of assessment or diagnostic errors, the client or society must pay the bill.

More Efficient Use of Social Institutions

In a republic where democratic practices and philosophy are important, we expect some lost motion and inefficiency. However, even in such a country there are limits to what the patience of the citizen or his bank balance will stand. The professional psychologist in educational or business institutions spends much of his time on problems which involve more efficient use of the institution and the distribution and adaptation of staff to special situations.

When we deal with the self-actualizing man or woman, the relationships to social efficiency are much less sharply defined. But they are there. Medical facilities, avocational and recreational opportunities, community projects, church activities, and the myriad other outlets for time and energy are to some extent related to how well each contributing citizen distributes himself and is distributed. Psychoevaluation which leads to greater self-actualization contributes to social efficiency. The concept of social homeostasis has application for this objective of our process.

Summary of Objectives

There is no compulsion to add goals and objectives for psychoevaluation to the above. One might claim with some validity that if the listed objectives are met, a contribution has been made to mental health. It is also probable that attainment in part of any of them makes a contribution to the adjustment of the client. For our purposes these, and other possibilities, are treated as unearned increments.

With one exception the intended loadings of the stated objectives are in the direction of better adaptation, self-distribution, and self-actualization of the mature, normal individual. Our exception, of course, is personal satisfactions and happiness. Here the emphasis is on internalized balances which are hoped-for results of the other objectives. Factors of personal adjustment are obviously a part of each of our objectives.

A PREVIEW OF CONTENT

PERSONALITY

In this preview of what is to follow, and in the specific materials in Chapters 2 and 3 which deal with personality and learning, no attempt will be made to develop new theories or greatly modify any one theory. As Hebb (1958, 259–260; see also 1958*c*, 456–458) has so aptly said:

> A man who constructs a theory is certainly trying to hit the truth, but the function of theory is better seen, perhaps, if we regard it as a sophisticated statement of ignorance: "sophisticated," because the ignorance is put in a form that shows us how to go about decreasing it. The function of theory is to guide us to new observations and better experiments. If it does this it is good, whether it is "true" or not.

No one theory of personality satisfies all psychologists, nor is any really intended to. Here we are eclectic and will be satisfied to string seemingly related hypotheses into (hopefully) meaningful concepts. At the level, and for the purposes, of assessment, trait and factor theory will supply a framework of hypotheses. At the level of psychoevaluation a soft determinism, tempered by our own peculiar concepts of self-actualization, will be followed. Attempts will also be made to bridge the gap between theories of personality and theories of learning at a molar level. We have borrowed, among others, from Allport, Brunner, Cattell, Darley, Eysenck, Guilford, Hebb, Hull, Maslow, May, Murphy, Roe, Rogers, Stagner, Strong, and Super.

In dealing with personality dimensions, the major problem is to interpret the theoretical research findings into language which will be meaningful to the client. To do this without serious loss or dilution of meaning is most difficult. For example, Cattell's *Universal Indices* (1957, 833–834) can, in some instances, be reduced to patterns or, as Maslow (1954, 31–37) calls them, syndromes.

Difficult as is the task, the desired results can be approximated. In a quite comparable manner traits, or relatively consistent behavior patterns, called aptitudes and abilities have been simplified for client use in such materials as the *Minnesota occupational rating scales.* A combination of these approaches which in addition introduce temperaments, sentiments, and attitudes will be found in Super (1957, 48), Guilford (1959), *Worker Trait Requirements for 4,000 Jobs* (U.S. Dept. of Labor, 1956), and Roe (1956). These relationships, and others, will be considered at greater length in Chapters 6 and 7.

LEARNING

Chapters 2 and 3, which deal more specifically with human learning, are not concerned with presenting, reviewing, or comparing the various theoretical positions of the learning specialists. In the first place, to the generalist the plural, *learnings,* appears more appropriate to the present conditions in the field than does the singular, *learning.* One does not brush aside lightly the group represented by the work of Hull, Skinner, Dollard, Spence, or Miller. But the author is just as cautious in the equally dangerous ignoring of Mowrer, Harlow, or Hebb. Persuasive as are the writings of these men, and others, there are reservations. There are many psychologists unwilling to agree that QED can be written at this time in the fields of human learning.

People do change their behaviors as an outcome of experience. They do store past experiences and use this storage as standards against which they can test their perceptions of new experiences. They do scan the filing system of the central nervous system in order to behave in complex situations in manners perceived as appropriate. They do learn roles which seem to come into play almost automatically as situations call for one role rather than another. But no one theory seems to satisfy all psychologists. And there is always the ghost of free will lurking in a deterministic background.

Because Hebb (1958*c*, 460) expresses the author's confusion about learning theory so nicely, this section comes to a close with a quotation:

> Let us be clear first that there is no possibility of a physiological psychology that can avoid use of "intervening variables" or "dispositional concepts"—conceptions that refer not to a specific structure, or activity of a specified kind in a specific locus of the nervous system, but to a property of functioning of the whole nervous system which is known from behavior and which must involve such complexities of unit interactions in the nervous system that it would be impossible to specify them in detail.
>
> It is not remotely possible to give an account of the simplest behavior of the whole mammal without making use of such conceptions. Motivation, learning, intelligence, emotional disturbances—we may hope to refine such ideas or to substitute better ones for them, but there is no avoiding terms at this "molar" level of analysis. For them we can give none but the vaguest of physiological referents at present; they must refer to modes or degrees of organization, not to specific structures or processes; and they must consist of fantastically complex interactions, both spatial and temporal.

THE CLIENT

Two chapters, 4 and 5, deal with the normal, mature, self-actualizing men and women whom we call clients. Chapter 4 considers them broadly in terms of the three dynamics and provides major categories into which many of these individuals can be placed. Chapter 5 is composed of illustrative thumbnail case studies. Both chapters involve some problems of word usage. Some readers may have been puzzled, for example, by the use of *normal* to describe clients. The older English meaning of individual social responsibility is used. English and English (1958) give as the first definition "conforming to, or not deviating from, the usual or average of the type or norm." The use in this book is not concerned with the average, or an idealized social image. If a man or woman can find subcultures in a society in which he can support himself economically, live without being perceived by one's peers as a biological or psychological threat, avoid frictions which require social protective action, and be reasonably adjusted, in that society we consider him to be normal.

The word *mature* was discussed earlier in this chapter in the section devoted to the objectives of psychoevaluation. The dictionaries afford a number of meanings for the word, none of which fit closely enough the general intent of this book. Allport's (1937, 213–231) description of maturity was used, accepting his broad criteria of varied autonomous interests, self-objectification, and a unifying philosophy of life. To judge another as mature requires clinical inference and evaluation, not assessment. But we are constantly concerned with the degree of maturity others show (as we perceive them), and much professional psychologizing is done on the basis of such evaluations.

Self-actualization has been encountered in these pages, beginning with the dedication. Here again the reader cannot go to a single source for the usage in this book. There has been borrowing, and acknowledgments are made to Goldstein (1939), Lecky (1945), Rogers (1951), Pepinsky and Pepinsky (1954), Maslow (1954), and Super (1957). Perhaps one should include Otto Rank and Taft (1936). But in the viewpoint of the writer we have had more pointed contributions for our purpose from Roe (1956), Terman, and Terman and Oden (1926, 1947, 1959).

Chapter 3 carries the load of describing and discussing the self-actualizing individual. Three criteria for identifying self-actualization are considered: self-judgments, the judgments of peers, and the evaluation of the psychologist specialist. The dimensions of self-actualization used in this book are presented. They are, in order of presentation: relative scarcity; chronological age; maturity; high level of efficiency variables; self-expression, independence, intrinsic vocational satisfactions; leadership; social and vocational multi-potentiality; performance correlation with potential; moderation in social, economic and political views and behavior; social responsibility and contribution; self-sufficiency; creativity. The stand is taken that some of the dimensions can be present to small degree if other dimensions are present in heaping measure.

Related to self-actualization, some consideration is given to hypothesized degree-of-choice-freedom for the individual. Of course, all humans face situations where there are, or are perceived to be, no choice alternatives for behavior. However, the nondeterminist assumes that although he must enter the armed forces because of the draft laws, he can choose among the Army, the Air Force, and the Navy. In some legal jurisdictions if condemned to execution, he has the dismal choices among ropes, bullets, electricity, and gas. Attention is given in this regard to the contraction in choices with increasing age—psychological as well as physiological restrictions.

PROCESS AND COMMUNICATION

Chapter 6 combines elements found in counseling, sensitivity training, and aspects of the relationship between a Ph.D. candidate and his thesis adviser. From the psychologist's standpoint, as has been indicated earlier, skills stemming from assessment, evaluation, and diagnosis are involved. Process is presented as a joint endeavor having the *with* predominant. Much process control is in the hands of the client. For emphasis, *with* is not to be confused as a synonym for permissiveness as it is used in some forms of psychotherapy. Permissiveness connotes a granting of privilege to a patient by a psychologist to behave in certain ways in an interview situation. Psychoevaluation depends much less on the interview as the chief vehicle of communication than does either counseling or psychotherapy. The likenesses to thesis preparation stems from the process of psychoevaluation being a careful, systematic study by the client of the most fascinating subject in the world—himself. He selected the topic, knows more about it in many directions than anyone else, has high motivation toward successful completion of the project, and controls much of what goes into the final product.

Communication is dealt with in much the same manner that books in psychotherapy treat the interview. Chapter 7 attends to six major vehicles of which the interview is but one. In a process in which client effort, in terms of hours of time consumed, is greater than that of the psychologist, there appears to be little need for a 1:1 ratio of client-psychologist time. Interview time for an average relationship is estimated to range from five to ten face-to-face meetings. Bibliocommunication, personal documents, transcribed recordings, nonverbal cues, records, and psychologist's written reports shift the communication patterns strongly away from only a series of talks.

PSYCHOLOGISTS, THEIR KNOWLEDGES, AND PSYCHOEVALUATION

There is far from complete agreement among psychologists as to what professional psychology is and should be. Chapter 8 presents the author's view of the matter. The general theme is that such terms as clinical, counseling, and industrial have lost meaning and might be discarded for more descriptive functional ones. There is consideration of graduate training programs, with some suggestions as to needs. There is a look at the shifting place of the Veterans Administration in the training of professional psychologists as hospital populations become older and present problems quite different from those encountered when the program began.

Chapter 9 deals with what the nonpsychotherapist professional psychologist should consider as essential among his competencies in working with clients, helping them by doing something for them, or acting as a social agent in doing things to them. Chapter 9 also serves as a summary of the book in some regards.

Chapter 2

GROWTH AND DEVELOPMENT: PERSONALITY AND LEARNING

In this and the following chapter, too few pages are available to attempt a review of the literature or to synthesize the massive bibliographies in growth and development or in personality and learning. Moreover, recent years have brought excellent materials which do attempt to distill the essences of thinking in regard to each. In the field of personality and learning, Hall and Lindzey (1957) and Koch (1959) are useful. Gough's (1961) review of Koch's editorial effort is an aid to perspective. Hilgard's (1956) examination of learning theory prior to that date is helpful.

Hall and Lindzey (1957, 548) condense the major dimensions of personality theory into a table which allows a panorama of areas in which theorizing and researching have centered. These dimensions are:

Purpose	*Unconscious determinates*	*Reward*	*Contiguity*
Learning process	*Personality structure*	*Heredity*	*Early developmental experiences*
Contiguity of development	*Organismic emphasis*	*Field emphasis*	*Uniqueness*
Psychological environment	*Self concept*	*Group membership determinants*	*Biology*
Social science	*Multiplicity of motives*		

Because this book borrows extensively from Allport, Cattell, and Murphy, a comparison of their greatest divergencies in regard to the above dimensions is extracted from the Hall and Lindzey table.

	Allport	***Cattell***	***Murphy***
Early developmental experiences	***Low***	***Medium***	***High***
Reward	***Low***	***High***	***High***
Contiguity of development	***Low***	***Medium***	***High***
Organismic emphasis	***High***	***Low***	***High***
Field emphasis	***Low***	***Low***	***High***
Group membership determinants	***Low***	***Medium***	***High***
Social science	***Low***	***Low***	***High***

High indicates the Hall and Lindzey opinion of strong emphasis; *medium,* moderate emphasis; *low,* deemphasis. All are judged high for personality structure, biology, and multiplicity of motives. On the other dimensions they tend to agree on emphasis, but not completely. There is no dimension where all three are judged to deemphasize.

Learning theory is incorporated with personality theory in the text. The justification for this is taken from Hall and Lindzey (1957, vii): "we are willing to accept any general theory of behavior as a theory of personality." Reference was made in Chapter 1 to what the writer considered as confusion among and between research specialists and professional psychologists. In Chapter 1 Hebb (1958*c*, 460) was quoted to indicate some reasons for disagreements and lack of communication. The complexity of the physiological problems was considered so great that we cannot yet accept closed theoretical positions about learning on the basis of present knowledge. Much of the research with animals is related to adaptive behaviors—overt and observable. Molar levels of analysis are difficult to study in the laboratory. Such terms as *motivation, learning, intelligence,* and *emotional disturbance* will be with us for some time to come. To describe man as an energy system does not explain him completely.

Some of the conflicts between professional psychologists and learning theorists were well expressed by Butler (1954) and Snygg (1954) in papers presented at the Kentucky Symposium on Learning. Butler (125–26) said:

With respect to the contributions of the domain of learning to research in psychotherapy, it is my conviction that at present learning theory as such is able to contribute but little to actual research on the process of therapy. It seems to me that this is so because, as I stated earlier, translations or reductions of therapeutic theory to learning theory will not, in general, prove anything save that sets of propositions are consistent, and the question of the actual denotata of the therapeutic propositions is not solved by the process of translation, although the translations may be richly suggestive. As far as I can see, the best use of the domain of learning can come from applying the experimental techniques invented in the laboratory to tap processes and abilities which are used in everyday life and thus may be substituted for the usual measures of social adjustment which are so unsatisfactory.

Snygg (1954, 130) was more blunt in his statement:

The sad truth is that, after 50 years of careful and honest and occasionally brilliant research on the nature of learning, the only people who can be proved to have received any practical benefits from learning theory are the learning theorists themselves. The very inclusiveness and complicated nature of our current learning theories, which make them useless to applied workers, have proved to be occupational assets to the learning specialists. They can, if they wish, make rather good professional careers out of attacking the weak points in one another's theories, much like the shipwrecked Scotsmen who made a good living by taking in one another's washing."

The critical comments of Butler and Snygg, although made almost a decade ago, are still heard. The criticism, of course, is aimed at the difficulties of using the results of laboratory experiments with animals for working with human clients or patients. However, there is lack of agreement also among and between the learning specialists. This is true in any field of scientific research and surprises no one. Mowrer (1960, 1960*a*) has advanced theoretical views which are more acceptable to many professional psychologists than, for example, Skinner or Hull. The flavor of Mowrer's departures from $S \rightarrow R$ orthodoxy can be sampled in his treatment of sin (1960*a*) and in the following brief quotation regarding emotions (1960, 307):

> Our assumption, by contrast, is that the emotions play a central, indeed an indispensable, role in those changes in behavior or performance which are said to represent "learning." The emotions are involved, first of all, in that they are strictly speaking, *what* is learned. Fear, hope, relief, disappointment—these we assume are the reactions which are most readily and importantly conditioned, to independent and/or response-dependent stimuli, they then guide and control performance in a generally sensible adaptive manner.

These comments and quotations, together with what was said in Chapter 1, comprise the major attention that will be given learning theory, as learning theory, in this book. We in professional psychology have done little either to present theories more appetizing to ourselves or to accomplish research which might demonstrate if, and how, the learning specialists are wrong. We might, for example, adapt the techniques of a popular television show, Candid Camera, in order to study certain aspects of reality testing. We might contribute to learning theory by certain not impossible experimentation with our communication media and their effectiveness on limited client goals. It is doubtful that learning specialists in large numbers will cease their present efforts or change directions radically in order to satisfy us. Some believe that counseling, psychotherapy, or other methods of communication with clients or patients can be optimally successful only if the professional practitioner does attend to the learning process and have at least a partial theoretical base in this regard from which to operate.

Our next matter of concern is the developmental course of the individual as he moves from birth, through the decades of *becoming,* into sowing and reaping periods of *being.* The counseling psychologists have concentrated on the first three decades of life in our culture, for the normal individual. Pepinsky and Pepinsky (1954), Tyler (1953, 1961), Hahn and MacLean (1950, 1955), Darley and Hagenah (1955), and Cottle and Downie (1960) present representative material about these three decades. For this reason we can move rapidly over the terrain.

BECOMING: THE FIRST DECADE

IN THE BEGINNING

Despite a recent bath, sweet-smelling powder, clean diapers, and a full stomach, the human infant is an egocentric, completely selfish, delightful, demanding, unreasonable, exceedingly lovable tyrant! His one concern at times appears to be biological survival, supported by homeostatic built-ins and conforming to the "old" Marine Corps motto, "The Hell with you, I've got mine." He has inherited structures and tendencies, latencies, an unbelievable capacity for learning, and a quite indestructible physical organism despite the dismays of young parents. On the surface he is appealingly helpless.

Although the inherited equipment is still pretty much designed for biological survival—relatively early physiological maturing to cope with the tyrannosaur and the saber-tooth tiger, the streptococci and the staphylococci—our Western culture has relegated these biological considerations to the police and to those who wield the scalpel, the hypodermic needle, and the capsule of chemicals. The child has the advantage of a phenomenal central nervous system, phenomenal chiefly because of the presence of the newest model of the cerebral cortex. He is unaware of either the ascending or descending reticular activating systems, oscillation, or damping, but he makes full use of the mechanisms however they operate or whatever they are.

Our young protégé moves along with a noisy arrogance until verbal symbolism enters the scene. Once the young human can substitute verbal symbols for things and concepts and begin armchair pilot studies of the future, he enters his own version of a personal space age. Such terms as conscience, values, goals, motivation, socialization, maturation, and self-actualization become increasingly applicable to him. And psychologists enter his life. Should he be unusually well cared for, a candidate for legal adoption, show signs of marked dullness or precocity, or enter a nursery school at an early age, he will find himself in the clutches of one or another kind of psychological specialist. He has been launched in the shallowest waters of becoming. The journey to the open sea of maturity will be logged as curiosity and exploration, manipulation, hope and fear, and vigilance are integrated into the developing unique personality structure. And the integration will be called learning.

By the end of this first decade of becoming, a quite firm foundation for the man-to-be or woman-to-be has been laid. Enculturation has begun and grown in the family and neighborhood group. Structure for social behaving has been partially rigidified by these influences and those of church and school. For many, the junior gang has been contributing somewhat less accepted social behavior added to, and incorporated in, the developing system. If minimally adequate sensory experience has been available with appropriate spacing, we can assume that sensory deprivation has not seriously impeded growth or limited potentials.

In this first decade differentiation of function has been rapidly effected. Constant practice with once novel situations is contributing to canalization, if one prefers Murphy's (1947) terminology, or programming if Bruner (1958) is the model. Cerebral nets and circuits have developed for memory storage which permit situational comparisons with new experiences. Increasingly complex symbolic stimuli result in more complicated responses, overt and covert, including integrated roles and masks. People are still doing things to him and for him—in the home, the church, the school. His peers in the various social groupings which he encounters do things to him and for him, but they also share more and more activities *with* him.

BECOMING— THE SECOND DECADE

In some primitive societies the child at ten years of age is very close to the day when he can say "Today I am a man." In our culture, until late in the decade, the effects of the industrial revolution and other factors have made these youths of not much economic consequence. Socially and economically dependent, but sexually quite mature, they very often present problems to which we tend to attach the generalization of "juvenile delinquency." With communication, particularly the motion picture and television, providing stimuli which their grandparents could not equal in a lifetime, the fear of general sensory deprivation is somewhat mitigated. Some problems may be those of too much rather than too little sensory bombardment.

Because this age group is institutionalized in formal education, it provides a captive audience for data collection and research. We are embarrassed by the sheer weight of paper needed to record and preserve our data and research hypotheses. Because we are hurrying by this age group, reference is made only to the longitudinal studies of Terman (1926, 1947, 1959) and his colleagues as a model of certain kinds of investigations. As the nature of our school lockstep shifts from a general orientation to the environment to verbal and other abstractions, the boy and girl encounter adults using the methodologies of psychology. The "sorting of souls" which occurs in our secondary schools exposes him to problems of adaptation, distribution, and adjustment which are increasingly more involved. Special capacities and potentials become apparent, and individual differences are more marked among and between himself and his fellows. Long-circuited interests can be detected which act as focal points for motivation.

Those youths who have begun to demonstrate behaviors predictive of self-actualization find that they have advantages in the social manipulation of others. External restraining influences are fewer, and the methods of evading or avoiding constraint are learned and practiced more rapidly. A recognized high level of the efficiency variables brings rewards. The joy of self-distribution in a number of directions is experienced. Ever increasing degrees-of-choice-freedom are perceived, sought, and achieved. For youth less well endowed, or with fewer opportunities for development, much the same process is in evidence. However, one may hypothesize qualitative differences in the fields and levels of activity between the potential self-actualizers and those who show less promise.

Whatever position one takes in the determinism versus free will area, the qualitative differences between individuals do appear to permit some a much wider range of "being determined." The number of alternatives, their quality, the forgoing of present smaller rewards for future greater ones, the goodness of reality testing—all of these among other considerations lead to at least an illusion of freedom of choice.

In the last half of the second decade of becoming, the majority of youths in the United States move into the sowing period of the decades of being. Although the average number of years of formal education for our citizens has moved steadily upwards, in many states young men and women can leave school at age sixteen. By age eighteen the compulsory school attendance laws no longer apply. At the time of this writing the school drop-out is being considered as creating a national problem. We have here one of the few quite sharp lines of developmental demarcation in our culture—the separation from formal education marks the entry into adult responsibilities. And the least able are among the first to leave school, find a job, marry, and begin raising children.

The more able, including the neophyte self-actualizers, tend to prolong the years of formal education and to assume adult status at a later date. It can be shown that this condition is highly correlated with the socioeconomic level of the parents and their educational attainments. However, the unaccounted-for variance is greater than that accounted for by these two factors. Heredity certainly is in the picture. One cannot rule out the effects of majority or minority group membership. Family, religious, and national cultures and subcultures carry a loading in many situations. "Self-made" men and women upset our generality. But the generality still has meaning; the more able prolong the period of formal education and enter economic competition later than do the less able.

Completing the period of *becoming* early is perceived by some youth as having important rewards. For example, the young man or woman has much more freedom from parental control. Social restraints appear fewer and less stringent. One achieves an independent income. The range for exploration and manipulation of the environment is increased. These rewards tend for many to be short-range gains. Mowrer's (1950) temporal contiguity of rewards and punishments seems to have application to the normal individual of limited potential as well as to those exhibiting neurotic behavior.

FROM WHAT THEY CHOOSE

Although we are approaching rapidly our major consideration of the normal, mature, self-actualizing individual, the paths of youth in general have crossroads some of which all tend to encounter. Quite early choices are made which have a strong influence on the life-styles and patterns which are taking shape. These choices include vocational direction, social settings, geographical location, recreation, avocations, marriage, religion, political affiliations and activity. *Value hierarchies* and systems become set at Cattell's sentiment level. Long-circuited goals are appraised and tested against reality. *Wants* and *needs* reflect the personal patterns of short-range goals.

Vocational Direction

The average emerging citizen—valuable, hard-working, solid middle half of the population—faces one general direction vocationally. The emerging citizen—potentially self-actualizing, high on the efficiency variables, committed to a longer period of formal education—faces another. The distinction lies in that between a *career* and a *job*. *Career* is defined in a standard dictionary as "A profession or other calling demanding special preparation and undertaken as a lifework; as to follow diplomacy as a *career*." Implied in this is the important matter of relatively late vocational decision, a longer than average education or special preparation, and a complexity of function which will have *intrinsic* personal values of a high order throughout the life working span. Note that the dictionary uses *diplomacy* as a representative example.

Job, on the other hand, carries implications of short-term, periodic shifting from one employment to another, a relatively short term of preparation not necessarily closely related to systematic or formal education, and less social status. Although a series of jobs often will be related in function—mechanical, clerical, physical agility—they do not usually constitute a career. In applying Gresham's law to semantics, we do label some job publications as "career planning." But what most people do for a livelihood is not a career in the sense the term is used here.

It is probably true that the life pattern of jobs reflects many personality dimensions which have meaning for understanding the individual. However, as is evident from the study of measured interests, the closer we move to the mean of the population the more difficult it becomes to differentiate among and between individuals in terms of special personality factors which fit one for A rather than B. Whether we discuss the young adult in terms of jobs or careers, the decisions which launch the working life are exceedingly important. The reader interested in an extensive consideration of vocational direction will find Super's *Psychology of Careers* (1957) an informative treatment of the subject.

Social Settings

Adaptation at times requires that we confine our social relationships in large part to those who work with us, live around us, and who belong to the social groupings with which we associate ourselves. There is evidence that people make these choices also in terms of "Birds of a feather. . . ." We are more comfortable with those whose attitudes, goals, and values are similar to our own (see Darley and Hagenah, 1955, Chapters 2 and 4). Whatever the causes and motivations of and for social self-distribution, the company one keeps is indicative to a certain extent of what we are and where we are going. Social self-distribution is a series of choices which can have important bearings on later life and its directions.

Geographical Location

Although filling stations and motels give the illusion that all places in the United States have become carbon copies of each other, localities and regions, like colleges, do have "personalities." Consensus attitudes and value systems vary from rural to urban, East to West, North to South, and from primarily agricultural to primarily industrial areas. Economic opportunities also vary along these axes. Life-styles are determined in part by geographical location. Clear examples are to be found in the migration of the Negro from the South, the Spanish American from Mexico and our Southwest to the North, and the movement of the Puerto Rican to New York City. Whether the new conditions are better or worse is a matter of opinion, but there is little question but that the conditions are different. And being different, the changed second dynamic is an important factor in making us what we become.

Recreation

Our forms of recreation are expressive behaviors. They reflect our chronological ages, sex and M-F balance, social settings, education, geographical location, and also important personality dimensions. Like avocations (Super, 1940), recreational pursuits may have a reasonably high relationship to our vocations. Although the second dynamic places restrictions on us, we do have a quite large number of degrees-of-choice-freedom in this area. Our value hierarchies and long-term goals can be reflected in these choices.

Avocations

To discriminate between recreational activities and avocational outlets is sometimes difficult. Recreation, for some, becomes avocation; and avocation, recreation. Vocation can become avocation and avocation, vocation. It is probable that avocation, vocation, and recreation all represent facets of the hypothesis that interests are an important focusing device for motivation. Within personal and environmental limitations, there are degrees-of-choice-freedom for most individuals relative to avocations.

Marriage

There may be general agreement that the choice of a wife or husband ranks among the more important life decisions. Whether such choices are made in heaven or in the marriage counselor's office, the man or woman's life-style and pattern is heavily influenced by this usually second or third life-decade step. Again, there may be many limitations on our degrees-of-choice-freedom, but, for the majority, some such freedom is present.

Religion

A majority of our youth who have become will have needs and cultural patterns which bring religion, with its beliefs and faiths, into the individual and family life. Many will continue to follow the conditioning and canalizations of the father's family and its associations in their religious affiliations. Some will make religious choices through marriage and others, by baptism or conversion. Some will turn to philosophy, morals, and ethics without adherence to any orthodoxy. Others choose to avoid making choices among and between these alternatives. But there are degrees-of-choice-freedom, and this decision may be of great importance to many throughout the life-span.

Political Affiliations and Activity

Political beliefs and affiliations, in a broad sense, are often "built in." Socioeconomic status and familial settings are partial determiners, as is geographical location. Allegiances and loyalties exist, or come into being, which often endure for the life-span. The causes we espouse, the candidates we support, the political party for which we expend time and effort—each of these categories tends to reveal personality dimensions which are subject to interpretation and evaluation early and late in life. We do have degrees-of-choice-freedom in our political loyalties and affiliations. And for many, these choices have an important bearing on future directions in life-style.

IN SUMMARY OF CHOICES

The preceding discussion of choices which individuals make as they move from the decades of becoming into those of being pertains chiefly to those between the ages of fifteen and twenty-five. In less complex cultures and societies, these choices are made even earlier. There is no way to know what differences would have been apparent in the life-styles and patterns of the middle-aged had some of these choices been of better, or worse, quality.

One might, in the United States, label this ten-year period of choices "the counseling age." A large proportion of those who bear the label "counselor" devote their efforts to this age group. Counseling psychology has made most of its contribution to those in this age group and the institutions which serve them. The National Defense Education Act reflects the belief of Congress that counseling services are necessary for those at an age when these important choices of life-long impact are made. As has been stated, there are excellent books, and several professional journals, which attend to those completing the process of becoming and entering the stage of being. Even more attention from the ADAPTATION-Distribution-adjustment psychologists is indicated in the years immediately ahead. There is just as obviously a need for the ADJUSTMENT-

Adaptation-distribution psychologist to be on the team. But the situation appears to demand these important professional people for a relatively smaller portion of the total number requesting services or having services inflicted on them—after all, 80 per cent of us *must* be normal.

Throughout this section the attempt has been made explicitly and implicitly to weave long-range goals and value systems into the discussion of choices. In a very real sense, the overt observable behaviors which accompany any of the choices considered can be regarded as manifestations of goal concepts and directions as well as the value systems. Whether it is logical, or psychological, to treat long-circuited goals and value hierarchies in a separate section is open to debate. The author has chosen this approach, whatever its shortcomings.

LONG-RANGE GOALS AND VALUE HIERARCHIES

Under this heading four terms related to important life choices are considered briefly. These are *values, goals, needs,* and *wants.* Although the terms are treated under separate headings, there is clear recognition that we cannot distinguish sharply as to when a need is a goal, a goal a value, or a value a want. The importance of the concepts lies in large part in considering them as rubrics which attempt naming complicated interacting forces simply conceptualized in a form such as Cattell (1950, 156) used to illustrate a dynamic lattice. Better understanding of Cattell's presentation will be found in a later book (1957, 490–586). Maslow's (1954, 80–154) discussion of some of the dimensions of values, goals, needs, and wants, although differing on a number of points from Cattell, is enlightening.

Values

Values are guidelines for personal and social living. English and English (1958) give as part of the definition of value "an abstract concept, often merely implicit, that defines for an individual or for a social unit what ends or means to an end are desirable—These abstract concepts of worth are usually not the result of the individual's own valuing; they are social products that have been imposed on him and only slowly *internalized*—i.e., accepted and used as his own criteria of worth."

Criteria for a value seem to include the willingness of an individual to sacrifice time, energy, personal possessions, and even life in order to follow his perceptions of the value symbols. Cattell's (1950, 156) sentiments parallel somewhat the choice areas discussed in the preceding pages. This parallelism is also in evidence in his revised list of sentiments (1957, 520–532).

Choices in becoming	*Cattell (1950) sentiments*	*Cattell (1957) sentiments*
Vocational	*Bank account*	*Profession*
		Mechanical-material
Social settings	*Country*	*Self-patriotic*
Geographical location	*Country*	*Mechanical-material*
		Patriotic
Recreation	*Hobby*	*Sports-games*
Avocations	*Hobby*	*Profession*
		Sports-games
Marriage	*Wife (family)*	
Religion	*God*	*Religion*
Political affiliations	*Political party*	*Patriotic*

Although giving names to values does not define them, it is of interest to note the titles used by Allport, Vernon, and Lindzey (1951) in their *Study of Values*. These labels are *theoretical, economic, aesthetic, social, political,* and *religious*. The overlap among and between values, goals, needs, and wants is found for example in Murray's needs (1938, 152–226), Maslow's higher needs (1954), Allport's interests (1937, 427ff.), and Darley and Hagenah's (1955, 103–133) discussion of interests and personality. Values appear to follow hierarchical order both for the social group and the individual. With aging the pattern of the hierarchy in the individual is subject to change, often without clear insight as to the timing of the change or the factors involved.

Goals

Goals are for achieving. If values afford learned social-living guidelines, goals are behavioral indicators of values in action. The concern of this section is not with short-term, directly achievable goals. Of more importance for the normal, mature, self-actualizing individual are the goals which promise major satisfactions in the more distant future and which provide minor satisfactions, as steps toward the conditions or acquisitions desired are perceived as successfully accomplished. Cattell's (1957, 189) *long-circuiting,* in which direct paths to goals are avoided (barriers) in favor of less direct ones, is of importance here. An example which includes this concept is the young man of eighteen or twenty who wishes to enter politics. Because he must support himself, the practice of law is perceived as providing both a livelihood and a flexibility of time use which makes the political goal more achievable. But he needs money to obtain his professional education and training. He also wishes to marry. Many such young men reach the goal, but not in a direct path or in a short time period. Barriers may cause frustration or deprivation, as well as further indirection in reaching the goal. For adequate treatment of Cattell's hypotheses, see Cattell (1950, Chapters 8 and 9; 1957, 568–572) and Hall and Lindzey (1957, 393–413).

Goals for the self-actualizing individual are many—short-range and direct, long-range and indirect. They may be pursued without a clear specific goal concept. They do not exist, of course, unless there is an aroused motive or drive. Generalized social and cultural goals can be named, for example, the labels used in the *Chicago Life Goals Inventory,* (1938). These are *security, personal satisfaction, service to others, prestige, financial returns,* and *power over others.* Here too, the relationships to value systems, social and individual, are apparent. The life goals of Terman's aging sample reflect the Chicago categories. When goals and value systems are in conflict, we may encounter Festinger's (1957) cognitive dissonance which in some ways parallels Cattell's (1950) dynamic crossroads. The motivational aspects of goals are of great importance.

Needs

Needs have had much attention in the literature. Murray (1938), Maslow (1954), and Edwards (1953) supply a representative sample of this literature. The concepts vary in a number of manners, for example, whether the term refers to a lack directly evoking action or whether it is necessary to assume that the lack produces a tension, and a resulting drive. Needs are often presented as synonyms for values and/or goals. Some usage makes them equivalents for interests. Maslow (1954) for his higher needs —belongingness and love; importance, respect, self-esteem, independence; information; understanding; beauty; self-actualization—appears to include values, goals, needs, wants, and interests. For our purposes in this book, needs are recognized but not emphasized. They will be treated as conditions subsumed under values, goals, and physiological and psychological survival behaviors.

Wants

"Man's needs are few; his wants infinite." The word is included here because it is found in the literature, sometimes as a synonym for need. English and English (1958) define want under *desire.* Synonyms given are *wish, crave,* and *desire.* It is considered in the dictionary as somewhat stronger than *wish* or *desire.* In the literature of measured interests and theories about vocational interests, it corresponds, in part, to Ginzberg's et al. (1951) fantasy period in vocational choice.

A SUMMARY OF VALUES, GOALS, NEEDS, AND WANTS

Value, goal, need, and want are dimension or category names under the general heading *motivation.* Avoiding a discussion of stimuli and their relationships to our terms as triggers for action, our labels have been used to denote partial determination of individual behavior and its directions. They have been used also as partial descriptions of personality dimensions which, under some circumstances, permit prediction of the individual's behaviors in specified situations in known social fields. Before reaching our destination in this chapter—interests as key, parsimonious motivators—one more detour is made. We consider now the efficiency variables: *aptitudes, abilities,* and *achievements.*

APTITUDES, ABILITIES, AND ACHIEVEMENTS

In the growth and development of the human personality through the decades of becoming, much depends on the inherited quality of the efficiency variables and the environmental opportunities for their development. Whatever the motivating powers of personal values and goals, performance which makes the motivation effective depends also on the *equipment* for externalized behavior in, and interaction with, the social setting.

Much of the research dealing with trait theory, aptitudes, and ability has come from mathematicians and statisticians. Factor analysis has been a much-used method. Mathematicians and statisticians are understandably reluctant to name the factors which emerge from the computers. However, if hypotheses are confirmed and theories emerge, many of their efforts are intended to be applied to people in practical situations. The communications of research psychologists are beamed to other psychologists. Even if a message signal comes in loud and clear to a colleague whose decoding equipment is appropriate, the secondary and tertiary transmission to clients and patients must be altered for receiving by quite different equipment. If, for example, the sending includes *cyclothymia, schizothymia, parmia, bimanufiability, threctia, adrenergic, casthenia,* and *zeppia,* the recoding to a layman is considerable. This is not, of course, criticism of the researchers. It is not their function to translate for clients or patients. The professional psychologist whether dealing with clients or participating in the training of graduate students does have the responsibility. And it is not an easy one to discharge.

The literature concerned with aptitudes and abilities is so profuse, and directed into so many special areas, that only a few mentions are made here by which the reader may familiarize himself with the subject. The developmental aspects of the broad field may be traced through Galton (1911), Hull (1928), L. L. Thurstone (1935), Bingham (1937), Spearman (1937), L. L. and T. G. Thurstone (1941), Super (1949), Cattell (1957), and Super and Crites (1962). Buros's *Mental Measurement Yearbooks* provide an ample ongoing record of the changing current scene. The Differential Aptitude Tests of the Psychological Corporation are an example of method. Terman and his colleagues (1926, 1947, 1959) have provided the story of long-term research. The Educational Testing Service, Princeton, New Jersey, is, like the Psychological Corporation and The National Merit Scholarship Corporation, an outstanding example of professional dealing with the efficiency variables in formal academic, and other, settings. Let us now turn to the major classes of the efficiency variables—aptitudes, abilities, and achievements.

Aptitudes

Aptitudes are abilities and abilities are aptitudes. Aptitudes are the potentials for present abilities to be organized into more complex or different behaviors. Bingham (1937, 16) states:

> Aptitude is defined in Warren's Dictionary as "a condition or set of characteristics regarded as symptomatic of an individual's ability to acquire with training some (usually specific) knowledge, skill, or set of responses such as the ability to speak a language, to produce music, etc." In referring to a person's aptitude for mathematics, or art, or carpentry, or law, we are looking to the future. His aptitude is, however, a present condition, a pattern of traits, deemed to be indicative of his potentialities.

The problems of dealing with aptitudes and abilities are not as simple as Bingham's definition might lead one to believe. The references cited above lead into statistics, personality theory, measurement, clinical inference, and a number of other difficulties. One of the greatest, as has been indicated, is that of semantics.

The chief impact of the research, teaching, and professional use of the concepts and constructs of aptitude, centers on the period of becoming. The crucial first two decades of life in our culture and subcultures are loaded with hopes and predictions. Parents, schools, business and industry, and the military—all are justifiably immersed in assessing the potentials of new generations. We attempt to identify potentials for academic, musical, artistic, social, and other socially useful and personally satisfying behaviors and to predict from these identifications the contributions to self and to society which may occur in one, two, or three decades. With problems of huge numbers confronting us, professional efficiency and speed are of the essence. When faced with populations numbered in the tens of millions, we cannot afford the time, personnel, or budgets for exhaustive attention to each unique individual. Assuming the competence of all who are minimally qualified as professional psychologists, we find not enough of them to take an idiographic, phenomenological approach to each citizen. Nor will there ever be, despite Boring's proof that someday there will be more psychologists than people.

We do continue to some degree to assess individuals as chronological age, maturity, and self-actualization increase. But assessment with its more specific and immediate goals has its greatest use in our culture with the young and those who are least self-actualizing. For those with general ability to cope with the environment and to maintain an appreciable degree of control in manipulating it, the more global processes of evaluation and psychoevaluation are usually more appropriate. The longitudinal record of adaptation is with these people available in the form of achievements.

Abilities

As men and women move further into the relatively long period of being, less attention is given to making plans for shaping the organism to perform increasingly complex or different tasks. Indeed, with our seemingly built-in resistance to change, when any large number of adult individuals is judged in need of major educational or vocational shifts, the situation is often viewed as a regional or national crisis. An excellent example of this is the attention being given to retraining workers whose present, or immediately past, occupations have been greatly altered or abolished by technological change, such as increasing automation. From age thirty on, we tend increasingly to travel with what we have acquired. This, of course, does not imply that we cannot change our behaviors through learning, but rather that we resist change mightily unless motivation is particularly strong. Fairly strong perceived threats to biological or psychological survival appear to be necessary to provide the motivation for marked voluntary behavioral changes in many of us.

English and English provide so comprehensive a presentation of the concepts of ability that it is quoted in its entirety as follows:

> **ability:** *n.* actual power to perform an act, physical or mental, whether or not attained by training and education. GENERAL ABILITY is concerned with all sorts of tasks, but especially those of a cognitive or intellectual sort. *Syn.* intelligence. SPECIAL ABILITY has to do with a defined kind of task. Each special ability should, when possible, be so defined as not to overlap with other special abilities.
>
> Ability implies that the task can be performed *now,* if the necessary external circumstances are present; no further training is needed. APTITUDE (which formerly carried implications of innateness) has now been specialized in technical writing to refer to the fact that the individual can be brought by a specified amount of training to a specified level of ability, either general or special, but usually the latter. CAPABILITY is the maximum effectiveness a person can attain with optimum training, CAPACITY is a loose synonym for APTITUDE, often with implications of innateness; it is sometimes a synonym for CAPABILITY (latter *prefd.*). TALENT is a high degree of ability or of aptitude. GIFT and ENDOWMENT are popular terms for high ability, largely innate. COMPETENCE is fitness either for a particular kind of task or fitness in general (GENERAL ABILITY). Ability is sometimes contrasted with personality but, in the broader sense of that term, ability is a part of personality.

If we indulge in free association and offer the word "ability" as a stimulus, "test" will be a not infrequent response. With younger subjects use of tests represents a common practice. As individuals become older, there is less tendency to rely on standardized test batteries and more on the life history and achievement records in special areas. As will be hypothesized in the following chapter, the greater the degree of self-actualization, the less frequently will the usual forms of ability tests be used for personal evaluation. These learned, genetically based, remarkably consistent behaviors which we call abilities are dimensions of personality developed in much the same way that values, goals, needs, and wants are evolved. Abilities do have a more apparent physiological basis, although a strong case is made in many theories of personality for a physiological basis for all.

Interests

Although professional psychologists, whether they specialize in adaptation, distribution, or adjustment problems, give lip service to the integration of personality variables in the mature individual, it is somewhat surprising that only a relatively small group has given specific attention to interests, particularly vocational interests. E. K. Strong and, in a different direction, G. F. Kuder have generally been given credit for the development and major research efforts in producing instruments designed to measure various aspects of vocational and avocational interests.

Achievement

Values, goals, needs, and wants provide reasons (motivation) for behaving. Aptitudes and abilities are the vehicles which carry motivation to ends. *Achievement is the record of goal attainment.* In our rapid journey through psychological growth and development, we have centered on the establishment of potentials and the long-range predictions for the individual's behaviors. Our young man or woman on entry into the decades of being has erected the rough carpenter's framework within which his personality and his life story will be completed by cabinetmaking, although some must adapt to more rough carpentry.

In Chapter 7, the life record is given attention as a method of communication between client and psychologist. Young adults do not, as a rule, have such records. They have not lived long enough. For these younger men and women, we depend on academic accomplishment and the evidences of successful social participation, usually also in an academic environment. But the records-to-be are important, and some useful predictions of future records can be made from the small sample of achievements-which-are.

INTERESTS

In this section about interests the problem of parsimony in motivational dimensions is the major concern. If all hypothesized dimensions of motivation were compiled by name and each was accepted as a relatively discrete force or entity, there is a suspicion that neither the analog nor the digital computer could keep up with the interrelationships. Nor does the positing of a single global motivator, such as a growth principle, leave us in a much more livable situation as practitioners, at least with the normal individual and problems of adaptation and distribution.

It is the conviction of the writer that what we call *interests* are the focusing "subjective values which are the core of the dynamics of behavior, and play so large a part in unifying the personality" (Allport, 1937). Although long quotations are generally to be avoided, the original discussions of interests as integrating phenomena are stated so clearly and well that they are used. Allport (1937, 427–428), Murphy (1947, 719–720), and Darley and Hagenah (1955, 191) are the sources of our quotations. Cattell (1957, 490–586) treats interests as important, but not in the same manner as do those we quote. We begin with Allport:

> No psychograph would be complete without some dimensions to represent subjective values which are the core of the dynamics of behavior, and play so large a part in unifying the personality. It is not necessary, however, to accept precisely the variables here proposed. Others might be preferred, such for example, as the four major types of occupational interest that Thurstone has distinguished, *viz.,* interest in *science,* in *language,* in *people,* in *business.*

The interests included in the present psychograph are five of the six "directions of striving" described by E. Spranger, and defined in detail in Chapter VIII. They can be measured with a single scale, and each nearly fits the normal curve of distribution. 17. *The Theoretical Interest,* 18. *The Economic Interest,* 19. *The Esthetic Interest,* 20. *The Political (Power) Interest,* 21. *The Religious Interest.*

In brief, Allport used as his dimensions of interest five of the same areas which appeared labeled as values in the 1931 collaboration with Vernon and the 1951 collaboration with Vernon and Lindzey. Murphy (1947) deals with interests as similar to dominant conditionings and hypothesizes overlearning as an explanation of their strength and duration.

The material discussed in Chapter 20 regarding the symbolic machinery of self reference warrants the belief that, by their early twenties, most individuals have stylized the schema of the self rather finely; a person resists changes in selfhood as he would mortal disease. *Interests* also behave like dominant conditionings. Data on the continuity of interests, which show a rather high degree of instability during the second decade of life, indicate that in the young adult this set of symbols has taken on (within the ordinary rather constant environment) almost the fixity—even the rigidity—of the fundamental language habits themselves.

The fixity of the self and of personal interests is intelligible in terms of the concept of overlearning. A task overlearned—practiced beyond the level of proficiency required at the time—does not readily extinguish. The language skills, for example, including typing and telegraphy skills, reach a certain level of proficiency which is highly resistive to the effects of disuse; although they may eventually grow rusty, they can be brought back to their original level with an almost infinitesimal amount of "refresher" practice. Interests—in work, in hobbies, in games, in books—are overlearned responses in this sense, and they stick, consequently they play a huge role in personality consolidation.

Darley, and Darley and Hagenah stress the same areas as do Allport and Murphy—the focusing power of interests where multiple motivators are concerned. They introduce also an emphasis given in this book—the need for semantic bridges between and among theorists, researchers, practitioners, and clients and patients.

For it is our major thesis now that occupational choice and measured occupational interests reflect, in the vocabulary of the world of work, the value systems, the needs, and the motivations of individuals. These choices, or measured interests are, in effect, the end-product of individual development and the bridge by which a particular *individual* pattern of development crosses over to its major *social* role in our culture. It is here, at the juncture of the individual and social definitions, that we are most handicapped by the lack of comparabilities of vocabularies; personality development in the literature of psychology is defined in ways not easily translatable into the vocabulary used in denoting and delimiting the tasks that make up jobs.

It is not by accident that English and English (1958) refer to *interest* as "a term of elusive meanings." Here we describe the long-range patterning of multiple motivating factors, or dimensions, in terms of a crude instrument the scores of which have yielded surprising consistency over decades and which appear to have a high relationship with external criteria of validity. Throughout the literature we find agreement that measured interests, chiefly in the vocational areas at the professional level, are fixed strongly during the two decades of becoming and remain substantially the same for the three to five decades of maintenance or being. Super, Strong, Darley, Kuder, Bordin and Tyler, as examples, have devoted much thought, time, and energy attempting such theoretical statements. Holland's (1962) formulations may bring us closer to definition. There is not as yet general acceptance for any one of these statements.

Our "crude instrument" is the Strong Vocational Interest Blank. E. K. Strong devoted an energetic professional life to its development. A comprehensive literature has grown up around the professional and technical use of the blank. Those who wish to read more deeply should review, among other items, Fryer (1931), Symonds (1931), Paterson and Darley (1936), Darley (1941), Strong (1943), Super (1949), Cottle (1950), Darley and Hagenah (1955), and Super and Crites (1962).

Although the blank has been revised, the twenty years since this was done has impaired its possible usefulness to an unknown extent. The first dynamic may have remained relatively unchanged. The world has changed, however, and the shifts in the second dynamic unquestionably have an effect on the validity of the scores. Although the present usefulness is great, there is need for a thoroughgoing revision of this blank, or, what is more probable, the creation of a new instrument. Should discussions regarding a new instrument bear fruit, it would more than likely be the result of group work rather than the herculean efforts of a single person. The costs of developing a new instrument probably will require the resources of a foundation or a test publisher with unusually large financial and personnel resources.

How much more successful the new approach will be in regard to including deliberately selected values, needs, and goals, and in focusing attention on the appropriate ranges of the efficiency variables, as well as on disposition rigidities, functional autonomy, dominant conditioners, canalizations, and programming, no one can predict. But it has been demonstrated that measurement is practical regarding interests, and the "better mousetrap" seems inevitable.

In summarizing interests, the most important aspect appears to lie in future developments. Although there are dissenters, the writer is convinced that E. K. Strong and G. F. Kuder, to a lesser and different extent, have provided instruments which have been amazingly successful in tapping consistent and durable dimensions of personality in the general area of motivation. The professional psychologist interested in the origins of these personality dimensions will find perhaps the best discussion in the literature in Darley and Hagenah (1955, 134–193). Tyler's development approach by means of longitudinal studies of children followed over a long time span shows promise. Holland's *Psychological Monograph* (1962) concerning typological investigations is challenging and should be closely followed. Cattell's and Guilford's ongoing factor analyses may help to clear the semantic confusion. Our youth leaving the years of *becoming* and entering those of *being* will be far better understood as the inevitable development of more adequate interest measurement occurs.

Chapter 3

PERSONALITY AND LEARNING (Continued)

IN THE LAST chapter the attempt was made to provide a brief hypothetical story of personality growth and development through learning and the modification of behaviors. The two decades of becoming adults, or at least assuming many of the responsibilities of adulthood, were treated as a period in which the nets and circuits of the central nervous system became increasingly programmed, or canalized. The hypothesis was made that situational frames of reference were established in memory storage, during the years of becoming, and that these circuits and networks provided the skeleton within and around which accretions and integrations of future learnings would take place. Room was left for major maturational and experiential modifications of the original framework. Attention was directed to the characteristic increasing resistance to change with age.

The problems of communication at various levels of psychological sophistication were considered. The needs for translation and interpretation from the laboratory and theoretician's desk to the ultimate consumer, the client, were stated. Determinism and free will crept in when choices were made about social participation, more advanced formal education, political affiliations, marriage partners, religious orthodoxy, and vocational and avocational pursuits.

Values, goals, needs, and wants were considered as multiple dimensions of motivation. The efficiency variables—aptitudes, abilities, achievements—were considered in their relationships as means to motivational ends. The chapter concluded with attention to interests as an integrative area for several important motivational dimensions.

The reader has encountered a number of concepts, constructs, and terms which have not been clearly defined. One of the most important of these is *self-actualization.* There has been some hesitancy in using this label because of its rather well-defined historical usage by organismic and social psychologists. However, coinage of a new term is not particularly appealing, and the synonyms available miss nuances which are desired. Even though the use requires some statements of "what it is not," as used in these pages, there is comfort in the realization that others who have used it have faced the same difficulty—for example, Goldstein (1939), Angyal (1941), Rogers (1951), and Maslow (1954).

SELF-ACTUALIZATION

Some individuals are quickly and respectfully recognized by others because of their abilities to cope with a wide variety of situational problems some of which are very complex. These same individuals usually exhibit also a high order of competence in manipulating the environment to their own ends rather than appearing to be completely controlled by external conditions and social forces. While it is true that these behaviors frequently are observed in a more or less specialized sphere of activity—social, political, or economic—they also are generalized over several somewhat different areas. Close social contact with such people leaves the observer with the impression of self-sufficiency and assurance in reality testing over a wide range of perceptions and with marked depth and penetration. These individuals may well be described as self-actualizing.

As we have done many times on previous pages, we go to English and English for a point of departure in the form of a definition:

self-actualization: *n.* **1.** (*A. Maslow*) the processes of developing one's capacities and talents, of understanding and accepting oneself, of harmonizing or integrating one's motives; or the state resulting from these processes.—The term represents a variety of data better understood when taken globally than when analyzed; it points to problems for the psychologist to study rather than to a problem solved.—*Approx. syns.* SELF-DEVELOPMENT (emphasizing the temporal evolution of inner unity), **self-realization, autonomy, individuation, productiveness.**

So far, so good, but our term carries accretions and protuberances from the usage of others. The first of these is a *growth* principle (Angyal, 1941; Rogers, 1951). As Pepinsky and Pepinsky (1954, 37) said of this, "It is one thing to point to regularities among behavioral changes in client-centered therapy and quite another to regard these as necessary consequences of a 'growth principle' or of a counseling approach that places the 'locus of evaluation' in the client." There may be convincing evidence of a built-in growth principle of the type posited in some self-theory, but it is most difficult to locate. A perhaps equally tenable hypothesis is that, since human needs are few, but their wants without end, those who manipulate the environment with unusual facility at a reasonably early age find that the number of satisfactions which can be had by effective manipulative methods increases with practice, and so with increasing chronological age and more practice there is "growth." Goldstein's (1939, 305) "joy of conquest" implies this kind of explanation. The question is also raised as to the period of life when goals and value loadings tend to change markedly for many. Does the growth principle continue to operate, and maintain itself throughout the life-span, or does it follow the decline curve of other motivating factors and energy supply and output?

Our second "is not" concerns the good and bad value judgments. If the outside lay observer supplies his judgments, these observations tend to match his personal perceptions and values. The professional psychologist should be much less prone to make moral value judgments regarding client behaviors, but if his mission is perceived as a cure or radical behavior change in the client he may be perceived as making them. If we rely on the individual exhibiting the behavior, our problem is the same. Nor can we ignore the possibility of genetic linkage in some behaviors that are socially and personally "bad." If we do ignore this last consideration, the position taken here would be neutral. Environment without doubt plays an extremely important part in what we are, and what we become, but the evidence that it is a single causal factor has yet to be demonstrated.

Goldstein, Rogers, and to some extent Angyal and Maslow, have considered motivation as a single, integrated force. There is no consensus as to how many broad categories, or relatively unique vectors of motivation, exist. Because of personal biases, the author's position is some place between Goldstein and Murray. Allport, Cattell, and Murphy, in this regard, are perceived as being nearest to the biases of the writer. Self-actualization is not conceived of here as having motivation explained by one or two "master" factors.

The last "is not" is concerned with explaining self-actualization only in terms of conscious states. Although moving a great distance from Allport (1937) toward Freud is discomforting, there is enough evidence to raise questions regarding the acceptance, or near acceptance, of conscious states as the only, or necessarily major, explanation of behavior determinants.

In summary, self-actualization will be described and used in these pages as not including a growth principle of the type found in some of the theories cited above. No value judgments of original good or bad appear necessary, unless they are made in relation to quite specific situations in a described culture or subculture. Even in such instances our good or bad must be in terms of the individual, society, or both. Motivation, then, is considered here as the integrated force of a number of personality dimensions including values, goals, needs, wants, and interests. Both conscious and unconscious motivations are hypothesized as being of importance in human behavior. It now seems advisable to move to a more positive statement of what we are considering.

SOME CRITERIA OF SELF-ACTUALIZATION

We look again at English and English's (1958) definition of self-actualization as "the processes of developing one's capacities and talents, of understanding and accepting oneself, of harmonizing or integrating one's motives; or the state resulting from these processes." The questions we must face revolve around "In whose judgment?" "By what criteria?" When we are faced with "the processes of developing one's capacities and talents," our psychological methodology for dealing with the efficiency variables—aptitudes, abilities, and achievements—comes into play. Here we tend to work in a nomothetic setting with Meehl (1954), for example, as one of our chief mentors. When we speak of "harmonizing or integrating one's motives," we move much more into covert, idiographic fields for criteria. "The state resulting from these processes" will tax our ingenuity as psychologists and, sadly, often outrun our competencies.

We call attention here to Pepinsky's (1948) categories which are discussed in detail in Chapter 7. His material has been restructured, and four of his categories—*lack of assurance, lack of skill, lack of information,* and *choice-anxiety*—have been labeled "normality indicators." These indicators have a rather heavy weight in determining the rough reliabilities and validities of our various criteria of self-actualization.

The Criteria of Self-evaluation

Men and women form images of themselves. These images are of many kinds, subject to change, and sometimes based on disparate conceptions of the self and reality. Some of the better-known professional and theoretical materials about self-images which may be of interest to the reader are those by, and about, H. S. Sullivan (1947), Alfred Adler (1935), and Karen Horney (1945). Although the concepts of "know thyself" are to be found in most of the theoretical systems concerned with personality, it is difficult to discover marked intertheorist agreement either in clear, commonly accepted names for the dimensions believed to be of greatest importance or in methodologies which guarantee reasonably high reliability or validity correlations.

In terms of self-evaluation we must face also the problems of the reliability and validity of self-report. Although Allport (1937) and Rogers (1951) have tended to rely more than many others on the usefulness of the data from direct oral or written self-reports, many psychologists are more cautious and less willing to accept such case materials at face value. Even though the psychologist is convinced of the sincerity and honesty of the client's statements about himself, Pepinsky's (1948) categories raise the questions "Does he have the skills to perceive and report himself and to understand himself and his environment?" and "Does he have the information to so perceive and report himself without unintentional, but serious, distortion?" (The reader again is reminded that we are not concerned with diagnosis or psychotherapy, but rather with the normal individual seeking better integration of personal and social dynamics.) Although we do not know the norms which the individual uses for self-evaluation of self-actualization, the evidence which we see every day indicates that a majority of us do such evaluation at a level sufficiently high to permit us to perform in consonance with our roles and their self-perceived statuses. This, of course, is no answer to *how much* self-actualization is present in terms of potentials which are not being efficiently used. It is probable that many people perceive comfortable, habitual levels of performance as being synonymous with maximal or optimal performance. In some of their self-images, they are self-actualizing to a great degree, regardless of the judgments of others.

This concept of *performance versus potential* haunts all of our efforts to clarify criteria for our terms. If the individual is completely happy with present performance level, feels no guilt or anxiety regarding personal or social responsibility for better performance, is above average in his social contributions, and is recognized as an outstanding community member, is he self-actualizing? If he is producing at ninety per cent of self-perceived capacity? Sixty per cent? Forty per cent?

Our discussion, of course, is aimed at the impractical attempts sometimes made to use a single criterion, not to discard data from self-evaluation. Self-evaluation and self-reports are necessary for any relatively complete consideration of a broad, ambiguous concept such as self-actualization. The reader will discover in Chapter 7 that rather extensive use is made of self-report in the form of personal documents in the process of psychoevaluation.

The Criteria of Peer Judgments

Although this source also is subject to distortion, we do pay attention to what colleagues and associates think a person to be when an evaluation of him is attempted. One of our most frequently used words in describing an individual for purposes of evaluation is *reputation.* Nevertheless, the psychologist knows that objective peer judgments are exceedingly difficult to obtain if the demand is made for data from unbiased sources. One approach to greater objectivity, for example, is to arrange for close associates to give such judgments by completing personality inventories in the role of the client.

In experimental situations, such as Murray's diagnostic councils, or various sociometric approaches, we do recognize the importance of using opinions and judgments other than those of the client and/or the psychologist. For practical purposes, however, few practitioners find many peer-contributed direct observations from which to add relevant data to their case files. One is aware, of course, that the individual is influenced in his own self-evaluation by his perceptions of his peer's reactions to him—for example, situational acceptance, ignoring, rejection, or isolation.

In the realm of inference the life history and various kinds of records give indirect evidence of peer evaluations. Reports of membership in organizations and attention to the types of organizations, their purposes and conditions of membership, yield cues and clues to better understanding and communication. The holding of elective offices may indicate the degree of acceptance accorded the individual in a subculture. Honors conferred by organizations, institutions, and governmental units often are excellent indicators of peer attitudes and evaluations of a man or woman.

The Criteria of Professional Evaluation

We have seen that the individual's self-evaluation is subject to distortion from the effects of seeing himself from "inside," and the difficulties of arriving at reliable and valid points for comparing himself with representative others. The judgment of peers, while valuable, suffers from the lack of reasonably representative norm points, inexperience in separating roles from masks, and positive or negative halo effects. The psychologist also has limitations in evaluating the self-actualization potentials and achievements of clients. At the same time his training and experience give him some advantages over the other evaluators.

First, the psychologist has a systematic and tested approach to identifying and assigning clinical and/or actuarial weights to personality dimensions. This permits a more parsimonious structure for evaluation. He has the advantage of generalized experience with the dimensions of cultures, subcultures, surrounds, situations, and fields with which the individual personality must interact. The client may be better informed than the psychologist about many aspects of the second dynamic, but he has this knowledge in a differently perceived phenomenal field.

Second, the psychologist has better access to the evaluations of both the client and his peers. Even though the peer information is most often from secondary or tertiary sources, the psychologist has methods of obtaining peer judgments which are difficult or impossible for the client to use, and he also has better methodologies for assessing these judgments. The client will give the psychologist data which the layman might not consider relevant. He will provide the information in a form likely to be most useful for process objectives when this form is stipulated by the psychologist.

Third, the psychologist must provide process structure even though the client is in control of much that is process content. Assuming that the process is an appropriate one and that objectives are usually met by following its organization, evaluation of the client's psychological assets and liabilities is in a perspective not possible for the client. The client is studying himself, but he does so through communication vehicles not within his accustomed coping repertoire.

We conclude our comments on the evaluation of the dimensions of self-actualizing by reemphasizing the difficulties. There is no consensus as to what self-actualization is. Agreement goes only as far as saying that there are processes, or a state growing out of these processes, which can be called self-actualization. We have no demonstrably clear and valid criteria for these processes. We have no particularly effective evaluative methods on which to rely when we make judgments about them. And yet, the author remains convinced that he knows and can identify a better than chance proportion of such people. He is equally convinced that his psychological colleagues are in a like state. In order that the reader arrive at his own conclusions in these regards, we next consider descriptions of selected dimensions of self-actualization.

SELF-ACTUALIZATION: A DESCRIPTION OF SELECTED DIMENSIONS

Our heroes and heroines—self-actualizing, normal, mature individuals—deserve a book entirely devoted to describing, analyzing, and interpreting them and their contributions to themselves and to their cultures. This book centers on other axes. On the following pages are presented selected personality dimensions and social behaviors together with descriptions of such people. Each statement (hypothesis) is surrounded by unstated qualifications and reservations which will be obvious to the reader. The positive nature of these statements should be interpreted as recognizing central concepts. Important discussion is sometimes omitted because of space limitations. The reader with special interests in any aspect of the material can pursue these in the reasonably rich literature to which he can turn for more intensive, and extensive, treatment.

The self-actualizing individual comprises 15 per cent or less of the population of the United States. (Terman and Oden, 1959; Darley and Hagenah, 1955, 29ff.; Maslow, 1954.)

The self-actualizing person will be perceived as such after age thirty-five. (Lehman, 1953; Terman and Oden, 1959, 144–49.)

The self-actualizing person will be perceived as mature. Although there are many definitions and meanings of the word *mature,* Gordon Allport's (1937, 212–231) description of *The Mature Personality* appears to meet our needs here. If one has "a variety of autonomous interests," "self-objectification," and "a unifying philosophy of life," he is mature enough.

The self-actualizing person will be a minimum of one standard deviation above the broad cultural norms of his national population on indices or ratios for the efficiency variables—aptitudes, abilities, and achievements. The evidence from so many sources supports this generalization that specific references do not seem necessary.

The self-actualizing person will have goals and values centering around self-expression, independence, and intrinsic social and vocational satisfactions. (Centers, 1948; Darley and Hagenah, 1955.) Terman and Oden (1959, 152) list subject-originated goals of a generalized "life success" as:

a. Realization of goals, vocational satisfaction, a sense of achievement;
b. A happy marriage and home life, bringing up family satisfactorily;
c. Adequate income for comfortable living (but this was mentioned by only 20 per cent of women);
d. Contributing to knowledge or welfare of mankind; helping others, leaving the world a better place;
e. Peace of mind, well-adjusted personality, adaptability, emotional maturity.

The self-actualizing person exhibits leadership behaviors in numerous directions and at various levels.

The self-actualizing individual is multipotential in his vocational, avocational, and other social roles. Noteworthy achievements will not always be congruent with the areas of his specialized, for-

mal, professional education. (Darley and Hagenah, 1955. See especially the discussion of the "professional trap.")

The self-actualizing person performs more closely to his peer and psychologist-made estimates of potential than is true of other normal, mature individuals. Individuals in our category of self-actualization are perceived to develop coping behavior early and to be unusually adept at controlling and manipulating environment in manners which afford greater scope for using their personalities effectively and efficiently.

The self-actualizing individual is a moderate in his social, political, and economic viewpoints. (Terman and Oden, 1959, 119–131.) While, as readers will point out, there are many exceptions to all the hypotheses presented, if we consider most of the Terman study sample individuals as self-actualizing women and men, this statement appears to hold as a generalization. He also appears to be a moderate in his gambling, drinking, and divorcing. Room is left, however, for quite a number of interesting vices and vigorous social dissents without his being banned from "the club."

The self-actualizer contributes proportionately more than others to his society. (Maslow, 1954, 217–224; Terman and Oden, 1959, 143–152.) There is nothing surprising in this hypothesis. An unusually good inherited structure, excellent early exposure to varied and relevant stimuli, early development of symbolic means for testing reality and exploring and manipulating the symbols for perceived reality, high status needs, and the well-integrated efficiency variables which permit outstanding qualitative choices among clearly seen and understood complex choices of behavior—all of these, and more, should surprise and astonish us if the behaviors did not contribute at a high level to personal success and to the social organizations and structures both qualitatively and quantitatively.

The self-actualizing man or woman is self-sufficient. (Maslow, 1954, 212–214.) Avoiding Maslow's growth principle as he states it, his hypotheses about self-sufficiency appear sound. Our subject discovers early in life that he has difficulty in being interested in, and communicating about, some matters which concern most of his chronological peers. He accepts the relative loneliness, and because his interests and many of his perceptions are relatively unique in the peer group, he is forced to depend more on his own resources. Once he discovers that he can trust his judgment and that, for him, the outcomes are more satisfying when he does, a major dimension is added to his life-style. He protects his time and directs his efforts in such ways as satisfy himself. The negative behaviors to which Maslow (1954, 228–230) refers may reflect in large part the defenses which the self-actualizer employs to protect himself from people—"he loves humanity," but people are thieves of time.

The self-actualizing individual is creative. Reference is made here to the exploratory and manipulative behavior of humans in our culture by use of symbols, concepts, and constructs. The ability to compare and categorize attributes of situations, and the complex fields within which the situations occur, while keeping in touch with reality, leads us to expect workable syntheses and novel solutions to problems in several areas of experience. Creativity is, of course, a relative matter. However, creativity perceived by the important others in the individual's value systems is characteristic of self-actualization. And the creativity may appear in any direction where efficiency variables and interests coincide.

In summary, at this point we have considered a number of dimensions deemed of importance in self-actualization which, to save reader time in referring to previous pages, are tabulated here:

Relative scarcity
Age group over thirty-five
Maturity
High level of efficiency variables
Self-expression, independence, intrinsic vocational satisfactions
Leadership
Social and vocational multipotentiality
Performance correlated with potential
Moderation in social, economic, and political views and behavior
Social responsibility and consonant contribution
Self-sufficiency
Creativity

No attempt has been made to supply point-by-point comparisons with Maslow's theories and hypotheses. It appears obvious that the dimensions we have considered will occur in varying patterns for each individual whom we may think of as self-actualizing. For example, one person will use chiefly the dimension of social responsibility and another the efficiency variables as behavior and performance indices. Some will elect themselves, others will be recognized by peer acclaim, and still others will be nominated by psychologists or other professional "experts." Some will be identified under two of our criteria, and a smaller number under all three—selves, peers, and "experts." In the matter of definition, we fail. Description has been our best solution. Nevertheless, there are self-actualizing individuals, and, for better or worse, our society must depend heavily on them for further social progress and for maintaining the best of what we have already achieved.

One more point is given emphasis. Seldom will an individual be found who has all of our self-actualization dimensions at an equal, high level. One can compare the situation to that of obtaining a high total score on a test with several divisions, or subtests. An A grade is awarded those who have a raw score of 75 out of a possible 100 points. If there are ten subtests, the total score necessary for a top grade could be obtained with an average score of 7.5 on each subtest. However, high total scores can be obtained by different patterns of subtest scores, and of individual items. There is meant to be no implication that one must possess an exceedingly high rating on each dimension discussed on the previous pages. In fact, one could imagine a very low level, or even complete absence, in one or more of the areas.

IDENTIFICATION OF THE SELF-ACTUALIZING

On the preceding pages frequent reference has been made to the samples found in the research of Terman, Terman and Oden, and Maslow. Maslow selected a sample estimated as selecting not more than one individual from several thousand. Terman approximated one in one hundred. The estimates used in this book are somewhere from one in eight to one in twelve. Maslow selected individuals ex post facto about whose self-actualization there could be little doubt. Terman's sample appears to include a small percentage of cases who did not self-actualize. Maslow selected after the fact; Terman predicted during childhood and early adolescence and validated his theories and hypotheses through continuous longitudinal life-style follow-up. What is considered in this section includes both prediction and after the fact. Two of our criteria are used—inferred peer judgments and the hypotheses of psychologists and comparable specialists.

The Period of Becoming—the Criterion of Specialists' Judgments

Public education in the United States has been characterized by pendulum swings from "traditional" to "progressive" movements. We moved in a period of twenty-five years from extremes of adaptation and distribution in the 1930s to the opposite poles of permissiveness and adjustment during the 1940s and 1950s. With the effects of Sputnik, in 1957, a swing in the reverse direction is detectable. Our heavy emphasis on the gifted reflects this swing back toward the thinking of Terman and Wood (1938). Focus on the efficiency variables is at the moment transcending our recent absorption with the feeling variables.

Examples of this swing are legion. On the national scene such organizations as the National Science Foundation, Educational Testing Service, Psychological Corporation, and the National Merit Scholarship Corporation, among others, are concentrating research and service efforts on those who show greatest promise for personal success and the attendant social contributions. Aptitudes, abilities, interests, and achievements are judged, estimated, and measured in order to select the best suited for further formal and informal education beyond the secondary school. In an era of national emergency related to foreign affairs, this is to be expected. Numerous colleges, universities, and public school systems have inaugurated the necessary local programs at the grass roots for the unusually promising.

If one looks carefully at what has been done, and is being done, there is little question but that our predictions of who will be self-actualizing are hearteningly sound in some areas of activity. One may judge from Terman and Oden (1959) that we have neglected to push as hard to identify early those who will be creative in the fine arts. It is true that the hierarchy of good traits will include some such potential contributors in any large sample. It is also true that we have not demonstrated that present tests of mental organization, and its quality, necessarily identify individuals with important special aptitudes and abilities in the areas of art, music, and literature. There is some comfort in the assumption that our pendulum will swing in this direction as the national and world scene changes.

One of our most disturbing problems in identifying the potential self-actualizer is that of the individual who shows the symptoms but who fails to continue the formal education which might make him self-actualizing sooner and at a higher level. Those in the Terman sample who did not go beyond secondary school could be used as a group with which to study a number of dimensions of self-actualization and its prediction in the period of becoming. For how many did the failure to continue formal education merely delay achievement? How do these individuals compare, when matched on relevant variables, with those who did continue formal education through college, and beyond, and have not been judged to have contributed to society or to self-actualization in line with psychologist predictions? What identifiable group and subgroup characteristics exist, if any? Are the exploratory, manipulative behaviors, at the time of prediction from test variables, hidden data resources for more discriminating inferences among and between individuals and samples?

The available evidence indicates that for the period of becoming psychologists and related professional workers can predict with some reliability and validity those individuals who will self-actualize in directions reflected in the curricula of higher education. Peer judgments may have relevance and self-images must be considered in noncurriculum directions, but there has been no convincing demonstration that these have the predictive efficiency of the professional psychologist's judgment in his spheres of special competence.

We have reached a place where unusually complete data are available to tackle the problems surrounding the prediction of self-actualization, however defined. For example, the University of Minnesota Student Counseling Center (Williamson, 1939, 1961) has files containing much information about the later stages of becoming. These data have been systematically collected and handled and date from the late 1930s. The publications of Williamson, Darley, Bordin, Sarbin, Berdie, Haganah, Layton, and a number of others give some indication of the richness of the Minnesota resources for follow-up research related to the prediction of self-actualization.

Comparable data are available for large samples on the West Coast in the files of the Student Counseling Center, University of California, Los Angeles, and at Berkeley. Here the files date from the 1950 decade. Beginning in 1957 at Los Angeles, research was done with gifted freshmen and high school juniors who entered the University as part of their program for the senior year. This has provided materials which are most promising for future planning.

Super's career studies, Holland's National Merit Scholarship researches on interests and their relationships to personality types, plus his reports on aptitudes and abilities—these and a host of less ambitious studies encourage one to predict appreciable progress in the near future. Terman, Terman and Oden, and Roe have supplied bases from which we can move further. Lehman's (1953) contribution on aging and self-actualizing and J. E. Anderson's (1959, 769–796) materials on the use of time and energy in the life-span contribute concepts and constructs which cannot be ignored.

THE PERIOD OF BEING

The task of researchers and theorists in the areas of predicting self-actualization has been relatively simple for the period of becoming. Our populations tend to be centered in, and about, educational institutions. Because educators and psychologists have captive subjects, a great many things can be done *to* and *for* them. The research and service tasks are infinitely more difficult (and expensive) when legal, economic, social, and political freedoms are attained.

Perhaps at the present time only Terman's data provide a reasonably complete pattern of life-styles through the span of becoming, being, and the early stages of having been. A great difficulty for researchers is that once men and women move into the thirty-forty decade, they almost disappear in terms of the behaviors that can be observed systematically by behavioral scientists. The breadwinners hide in a bewildering number of occupational labels. The homemakers are difficult to reach—even for a Kinsey. Our psychometric devices, with some exceptions when the chief concern is problems of adjustment, are not normed adequately for a population in this age group. Nor is there any convincing evidence of a large number of appropriate instruments for them. There are, of course, situations, such as World War II, in which large samples in this age group are available and subject to data collection for experimental purposes. However, "the good of the service" dictates the kinds of data collected and the methods which can be used for accumulating and processing those data. While psychologists often are in charge of business and industrial personnel programs at the professional and technological levels, they do not always have enough freedom in the design of general experiments. The chief objective of business, industry, and military is adaptation and distribution, and the professional modal methodology tends to be assessment.

Growing out of studies of military data, we do have researches such as those of Naomi Stewart (1947) and Thorndike and Hagen (1959). While such material is helpful in studying the thirty-forty age group, there is little in it which reflects directly on the problems of the mature, self-actualizing individual in civilian life. We encounter lack of appropriate experimental design for our ends. The relevant dimensions and patterns of personality for wartime military use do not coincide too well with the ones for our purposes, and unless a post-military follow-up of individual cases is made, it is not possible to identify self-actualizers. Studies like those of Block and Peterson (1954) have more relevance, but one hundred Air Force officers do not constitute a reasonable general sample for this age group.

In all probability, there are rich resources about this age group in the files of the numerous industrial consultants. Here, however, we are faced with the practical limitations which industrial consultants come up against when they work with private business and industry. Consulting firms do not publish much of their research findings, in part, because their contracts often specify that release can be only with the consent of the customer. It appears probable that, although the general approaches of industrial psychologists are similar, the specific psychometric instruments each uses differ. There is also the vexing problem of the communality of personality dimensions from study to study and the always present semantic problems.

The Period of Sowing

Because of our concern with a highly selected population, the self-actualizers, our period of "sowing" differs, for example, from Super's (1957). Super is concerned with the generality of normal individuals including the self-actualizers, but not concentrating on them (1957, 69–146). His materials begin the sowing period of being at the time of job entry after completing a secondary school education or dropping out prior to the achievement of this educational level. We are concerned primarily with those who are represented better by Lehman's (1953) subjects. The age ranges of sowing for this sample are estimated to be 25 to 40 in science, 25 to 45 in certain areas of the fine arts, 25 to 50 in literature, and 40 to 70 for leadership in education, politics, and law. Data from business and industry are not so clear-cut but probably follow the same general patterns along axes defined by the complexity of job functions and the demands for speed, originality, and creativity as against deliberation, information, and judgment.

If we use Maslow's (1954, 123–154) need hierarchy as a first point of reference, we find our self-actualizing young man and woman involved in marriage as the specific biological and social implementation of *the need for belongingness and love.* For the young wife, the family and the wife-mother roles become the foci for Center's (1948) self-expression, independence, and challenging work. For the homemaker, although Maslow's higher needs have meaning, there is a period of time when the career aspects so characteristic of the career woman and the male are submerged and do not act as strong motivators or disintegrators. They tend to reappear in force for the self-actualizing woman at some place in the second, or even the third, decade of being. This does not mean that the first ten or fifteen years of being are not years of sowing for the homemaker. Learning and personality integration are going forward in step with those who compete on the economic battlefields. When the inevitable research becomes available for this sample, we may understand the processes better. Because our self-actualizing homemaker will be considered at greater length in the two following chapters devoted to clients, we end our discussion of her at this point.

The career woman and the male enter a different broad environment and new subcultures as they drive toward what Maslow (1954, 27–28) calls the "*need for importance, respect, self-esteem, independence.*" The personality structure framework roughly constructed during the previous decades is exposed to processes of refinement and completion. Marriage has introduced the goals of providing shelter, food, sexual satisfactions and fulfillment, belongingness and love, not only for the self but also for "the important others." For the self the competitive drives, wants, and needs, involving the endocrine glands as well as learned behavior, integrate and push toward the "need for importance, respect, self-esteem, independence." The organism with its evolved equipment for meeting a hostile physical world must rechannel its coping behavior through innately inappropriate structures. In our Western culture we seem to invest the career with its status symbols and greater promise of security for the individual, his family, his community, and his country, with a strong concentration of cultural mold traits at the sentiment level. The wife, and later the family, become deeply involved and identified in this career focus, helping father to slay symbolic dinosaurs and cave bears.

The junior executive moves toward senior status. The M.D. shingle comes down as father joins a clinic and perhaps heads his own hospital. The school board member becomes a city councilman, state senator, governor, and sometimes a United States senator. For the one or two in a century, the American dream, log cabin to White House, comes true. Instructors become assistant, associate, and full professors. The artist for the college paper holds his first formal show, and the price of his artistic efforts mounts. The soprano from the mixed glee club arrives at the Metropolitan. The chap who, with his wife, started a roadside hamburger shop extends his chain of restaurants along hundreds of miles of nonaccess highway.

We believe that Lehman's conclusions are sound regarding what happens in that period of being which we have labeled sowing. New directions are explored. The effective stimulus-response level rises to a high plateau. Situational frames of memory reference increase in number and complexity. Appropriate responses are learned, and practiced, to an amazing number of situational and field stimuli. In the career area the learning and constant practice provide overlearning which gives the individual the sureness of action and security in meeting the demands of the second dynamic. His place in the pecking order of his social half-generation turtle shell is established in various contexts—the career specialty, the church, the golf course, politics, and at the poker table. By age forty-five, his major creative contributions are in, his reputation has been established, and he can reap what he has sown.

The Period of Reaping

The period of reaping is applied to approximately the last half of the period of being—thirty to senility. The business man or woman can show the results of successful enterprise in the form of prestige position, financial security, philanthropic contributions, and social and political power. The labor leader has regional or national stature and influence. The scientist has books, articles, membership in learned societies, and high academic status. The artist, musician, and writer can display the scars from the critics, the sales figures from distributors of the products, and look forward to further creative efforts. It is not a time for resting on the oars, but a time to continue being under less pressing circumstances.

Terman and Oden (1959, 145) report so well on important aspects of the reaping period of being that we quote—ladies first!

The occupations and occupational status of the men and women of the gifted group have been evaluated separately since the pattern in this regard has been so different. The careers of women are often determined by extraneous circumstances rather than by training, talent, or vocational interest. Whether women choose to work and the occupations they enter are influenced by their own attitudes and by the attitudes of society toward the role of women. These attitudinal factors also influence the opportunities for employment and for advancement. But in spite of the fact that American women on the average occupy positions of lesser responsibility, opportunity, and remuneration than do men, the gifted women have a number of notable achievements to their credit, some of which have been described in Chapter VII. That 7 women should be listed in *American Men of Science,* 2 in the *Directory of American Scholars,* and 2 in *Who's Who in America,* all before reaching the age of 43, is certainly many times the expectation from a random group of around 700 women. Publications of the gifted women include 5 novels; 5 volumes of poetry and some 70 poems that have appeared in both literary and popular journals; 32 technical professional or scholarly books; around 50 short stories; 4 plays; more than 150 essays, critiques, and articles; and more than 200 scientific papers. At least 5 patents have been taken out by gifted women. These figures do not include the writings of reporters and editors, nor a variety of miscellaneous contributions.

So much for the distaff side with its impressive record despite the onerous duties of "wifing" and "mothering" husbands and children. The male record is equally impressive (Terman and Oden, 1959, 145–147).

As for the men, close to three and a half decades after selection solely on the ability to score in the top one percent of the school population in an intelligence test, we find 86 percent in the two highest occupational categories: I, the professions, and II, the semiprofessions and higher business. Eleven percent are in smaller retail business, clerical, and skilled occupations. Farming and related occupations account for nearly 2 percent and the remaining 1 percent are in semiskilled work. The representation in the two highest groups is many times their proportionate share, with a corresponding shortage of gifted representation in the middle occupational levels. No gifted men are classified in the lower levels of the occupational hierarchy (service workers and slightly skilled or unskilled laborers), whereas 13 percent of the total urban population are in these categories.

Some idea of the distinction and versatility of the group may be found in biographical listings. In addition to the 70 men listed in *American Men of Science,* 10 others appear in the *Directory of American Scholars,* a companion volume of biographies of persons with notable accomplishments in the humanities. In both of these volumes, listings depend on the amount of attention the individual's work has attracted from others in his field. Listings in *Who's Who in America,* on the other hand, are of persons who, by reasons of outstanding achievement, are subjects of extensive and general interest. The 31 men who appear in *Who's Who* include a physicist who heads one of the foremost laboratories for research in nuclear energy; an engineer who is a director of research in an aeronautical laboratory; a landscape architect; and a writer and editor.

Additional evidence of the productivity and versatility of the men is found in their publications and patents. Nearly 2000 scientific and technical papers and articles and some 60 books and monographs in the sciences, literature, arts, and humanities have been published. Patents granted amount to at least 230. Other writings include 33 novels, about 375 short stories, novelettes, and plays; 60 or more essays, critiques, and sketches; and 265 miscellaneous articles on a variety of subjects. The figures on publications do not include the hundreds of publications by journalists that classify as news stories, editorials, or newspaper columns, nor do they include the hundreds, if not thousands, of radio, television, or motion picture scripts. Neither does the list include the contributions of editors or members of editorial boards of scientific, professional, or literary magazines. There have also been a sizable number of scientific documents reporting studies in connection with government research which are restricted publications. We do not have information on the exact number or content of these.

But the period with all of its rewards contains seeds of discontent. Time, which seemed without end a few years earlier, has become finite. Younger men and women are beginning to crowd into the competitive economic, political, and social arenas. To be sure security has been attained, at least to a minimally appropriate level, in the forms of material possessions, position and status, and in an ongoing career with productive years ahead. Retirement income has been assured in one or more of several ways. The family has been raised and launched into the late stages of becoming or the early stages of being. The home, the establishment of which was so strong an incentive in the first decade of becoming, has changed its character and acquired different meanings. Some activity goals have altered direction and others have been discarded, or at least contracted. The accustomed high level of stimulus need remains, but both because of changes in the individual and the work environment, response levels no longer match their former quantity or always, their former quality.

From the top of the mountain all roads lead downward. The epilogue of being is the prologue of having been. The striving, creating, purposive dreaming, and goal seeking of the sowing period have led to the fruitful years of reaping. But the urge to be a career and social architect and contractor is more or less gradually changing to the less taxing maintenance and upkeep of something attained and owned. In a very important sense self-actualizing people are at a stage for planning, for matching what they are becoming with what there is for them to contribute in a changing world.

J. E. Anderson (1959, 793) has summarized the problems of the last half of the period of being admirably when he says:

Obviously, this picture is affected by the social background and the cultural values of our society. In some societies individuals are perfectly willing to watch the time go by, but in our society, with its strong emphasis upon achievement and upon striving during the major portion of the adult life, the proportion of persons who fall into this classification is small. We then need to think of the older individual as a collection of attitudes built over a long period which regulate the manner in which he spends his time. If these attitudes have been built in a work-oriented society in which idleness, recreation, and leisure are considered a waste of time and hence are centers about which guilt feelings develop, the problem of the older person who is suddenly freed from time and space demands and has to learn to waste time rather than use it becomes an acute one from the standpoint of emotionality and of personality.

Chapter 4

THE CLIENT

BUT ONE practical difference between being good and being sinful is that the former is more tiring. In the middle of the Middle Ages, people of means and leisure suffered from a mental disease known as *taedium vitae,* a melancholy in which nothing seemed worthwhile, neither war nor love, money nor fame. There were various means of escape from it. The most civilized place in Europe was the Court of Burgundy and there men and women spent their time in elaborating a Court ritual that had to be meticulously observed every day. At other times immense banquets were given with surprises and entertainments which strike us now as jejune. One has survived in a nursery rhyme:

> "Four and twenty blackbirds were baked in a pie.
> When the pie was opened
> The birds began to sing,
> Oh, what a dainty dish to set before the king!"

It was scarcely dainty, but it *was* set before the ruler. The pie was enormous and the "blackbirds" were singers and musicians who emerged from it when the crust was broken, and performed. Elsewhere in Europe, men played complicated games of knights and ladies. In these, courts of "lovers" (who were forbidden to make any love at all) met to draw up rules for being enamoured and tried "offenders" against them, sentencing them to perform tasks for their ladies. But such frippery could not be called artistic and the people who wasted their time on them were not cultured. They were refined, perhaps, but that is a different, and a dreadful thing. (Menen, 1960, 126–131.)

Whether the first, second, and third dynamics are constants in time, or history is repeating itself, *taedium vitae* still plagues us in the Western culture. One has only to observe and talk with travelers in the hotel lobbies of London, Lisbon, Rome, New Delhi, or Tokyo, and the point is made. True, the Court of Burgundy is not replicated, but we seem only to have substituted the lure of the travel brochure and the world tour for the pie and the blackbirds. Men and women, having ridden on the merry-go-round a hundred or a thousand times, are aware now, not so much of the music and the motion, but that the left eye of the green swan in the inner row needs replacement. Having overlearned the appropriate complex stimuli roles and responses of our personalized life situations and fields, and having accomplished this overlearning in comparatively restricted aspects of life, in the years of reaping many seem to have lost some of the exciting exploratory and manipulative tendencies which made living the adventure it was a few years before.

With the emphasis which has been placed on the normal, mature, self-actualizing individual in Chapters 2 and 3, the question arises, do these people need consultation with a psychologist? The simplest answer is that *they do seek such consultation.* Aside from the personal experiences that many psychologists are constantly exposed to, consultation is sought. We see evidences of the felt need in the enrollments for the high level adult education offerings by colleges and universities; the attendance at lectures, symphony concerts, art displays, and intimate theater; and the amazing development of "do it yourself" projects and hobby facilitators, often at highly technical or scientific levels. Carl Jung, in an interview on his eighty-fifth birthday, expressed our thoughts well when he said (Young, 1960):

> For a long time I have advocated schools for the adult. It is when you approach the ominous region around the 40th year that you look back upon the past. . . . Inexorably a change imposes itself, subtly at first but with ever-increasing weight. Whatever you have acquired hitherto is no longer the same as you regarded it when it still lay before you.

For purposes of continuity, let us take one more backward look at the paths our clients have been over. When one was not yet thirty, forty was an unthinkable distance into the future. When thirty was passed, forty rushed on with terrifying speed. "Life may begin at forty," but it is the beginning of a period which, for many of them, is at least as new and anxiety-arousing as the break which occurred when they left their parental homes and assumed adult responsibilities. While we have labeled the years after forty as the decades of *being,* particularly with reference to *reaping,* we reiterate that these decades are also years of reaching and starting the descent from a summit. A few will descend only to a saddleback and use it to start up still another, perhaps higher, mountain. More will seek gradual downward paths which permit movement slow enough for attending to, and savoring, things and experiences which they missed in the earlier mad rush of the upward climb.

But whatever paths, there are new decisions, new goals, and shifted values to be considered. Many earlier goals—success, family formation and maintenance, home ownership, travel, relative financial security, parenthood, and for some, grandparenthood—have been attained. Values have shifted—they have had their thousandth ride on the merry-go-round and are eyeing the Ferris wheel. The points and frames of reference for reality testing have shifted. The words "probably," "possible," and "unlikely" have different meanings. Those who willingly gave hostages to fortune, took long chances, and played hunches now have moved from the one-hundred-dollar windows to the five- and two-dollar counters if they bother to go to the races at all. With this general overview of the maturing and aging clients, we can now focus on a close-up.

BEING

THE THIRTY-FORTY DECADE

The sowing period was discussed at some length in Chapter 3. In this chapter we look at much the same data and concepts in a somewhat different frame of reference. The self-actualizing person is in many ways moving through what will be perceived later by many as a golden age. Curiosity, exploration, and manipulation of increasingly complex situations, and field environment, give rein to fruitful and sometimes frantic activity. As competence is increased, and recognized, numerous choices must be made relative to career, social status, financial returns, recreation, power, and personal satisfaction. Clocks and calendars provide too little time for all that seems important and, regretfully, constrictions in activity are forced in the light of the individual's personality structure. It is in this crucible that Allport's (1937) autonomous interests and unifying philosophy of life are purified and can be seen in their proper context of the mature individual.

In general, this is a period of good physical and mental health. The physical organism causes little serious, immediate trouble. Commitment to institutions for mental disturbances is at a low ebb. Resort to the psychotherapist or the other professional practitioners in psychology is the exception. If the man or woman is engaged in business or industry, he or she may encounter the psychologist who acts in a staff or consulting relationship to the employing organization. Such relationships tend to be perceived as aids or barriers to horizontal or vertical movement in the career situation. For the self-actualizing the possibility of downward movement is seldom perceived as an important factor.

The period is also marked by the rapid learning of new roles for purposes of adaptation and distribution. In the arena of business and industry, Becker and Strauss (1956) provide sensitive insights into the importance of, and need for, the acquisition and polishing of many roles in the process of becoming mature:

A frame of reference for studying careers is, at the same time, a frame for studying personal identities. Freudian and other psychiatric formulations of personality development probably overstress childhood experiences. Their systematic accounts end more or less with adolescence, later events being regarded as the elaboration of, or variations on, earlier occurrences. Yet central to any account of adult identity is the relation of change in identity to change in social position; for it is characteristic of adult life to afford and force frequent and momentous passages from status to status. Hence members of structures that change, riders on escalators that carry them up, along, and down, to unexpected places and to novel experiences even when in some sense foreseen, must gain, maintain, and regain a sense of personal identity. Identity "is never gained or maintained once and for all." Stabilities in the organization of behavior and of self-regard are inextricably dependent upon stabilities of social structure. Likewise, change ("development") is shaped by those patterned transactions which accompany career movement. The crises and turning points of life are not entirely institutionalized, but their occurrence and the terms which define and help to solve them are illuminated when seen in the context of career lines. In so far as some populations do not have careers in the sense that professional and business people have them, then the focus of attention ought still to be positional passage, but with domestic, age, and other escalators to the forefront. This done, it may turn out that the model sketched here must undergo revision.

Kubie (1956) speaks for the scientist:

Certainly the idyllic picture of the innocent, childlike scientist who lives a life of simple, secure, peaceful, dignified contemplation has become an unreal fantasy. Instead, the emotional stresses of his career have increased to a point where only men of exceptional emotional maturity and stability can stand up to them for long, and remain clear-headed and generous-hearted under such psychologically unhygienic conditions. Thoughtful educators are beginning to realize that the socio-economic basis of the life of the scientist must be entirely overhauled; that the psychological setting of his life needs drastic revision; and that at the same time the emotional preparation for a life of research is at least as important as the intellectual training.

As part of the first dynamic, relative to knowing oneself, we assume that the insight of the sowers is at least adequate. Progress toward goals in a setting of personal values permits us to infer that our perceptions, including self-images, and societies' consensus reality are in reasonable accord. Problems of adjustment always accompany social adaptation of a complex nature. But these people being self-sufficient are also quite self-adjusting; and for this reason we assume that most of these problems can be handled within the resources of the individual, although at times with minimal adequacy. How much sound personal counseling, or psychotherapy, would add to happiness or efficiency we do not know. In most instances our individual muddles through without professional help for his adjustment difficulties.

His knowledge of the second dynamic situations, environment, and field may be somewhat restricted but ample for present needs. Use of this knowledge seems to be a matter of reasoning by analogy from previous learning, in the form of situational frames of reference, and incorporating new percepts, concepts, and constructs within the structure framework, often at a highly symbolic level. The second dynamic is concerned with sophisticated exploration and manipulation of the environment sometimes with new variables, but always loaded with syntheses and the formation of different patterns of behavior from previously learned materials. Help is obtained from senior mentors, colleagues, the family, and other sources in testing reality. There is little evidence to show how much use is made of professional workers, psychologists, or others.

The third dynamic—the interaction of the first and second—must also be inferred from broad behaviors and evaluation against the three criteria for self actualization. Certainly the perception and understanding of oneself in relation to the environment is an important dimension in being a mature individual. Our self-sufficient, creative, growing young men and women might use more attention from developmental psychologists, social psychologists, and those dealing with them as individuals in professional practice. Whether they receive this attention is not completely relevant. They have done pretty well without our ministrations.

BEING

THE FORTY-SIXTY DECADES

Reaping can be a most pleasant and rewarding process, period, and occupation. But when the harvest is under control, thought must be directed to the next season—preparation for a new sowing and reaping—and this belongs in great part to the next generation. Super's (1957) "plateau of maintenance" covers this period for our self-actualizers.

Again recapitulating Chapter 3 in part, perception of the time element has changed, gradually but sharply. Time is finite and to be measured against actuarial tables. The values and goals which provided strong motivation during the sowing period have changed in shape and degree of urgency. The pattern of interests is refocusing. Its general form is the same, but there has been some shift of emphasis. In short, time, which, like fire, is a wonderful friend and ally under the right circumstances is beginning to threaten as a potential enemy. True, it is over the horizon in the early years of reaping, but the dust of its march is visible.

The skills, knowledges, assurances, and sure hand in making important choices have been overlearned in the form of roles and their related behaviors for coping with the competitive environment of sowing. But this overlearning for one structure of goal pattern is not necessarily appropriate or satisfying when the goal pattern changes. What are the substitutes for mating, family rearing, security, rising status, and relatively successful economic and social competition?

Burgess (1960, 293–303) presents one schema of preparation for the problems of filling time. We quote from him as follows (295–296):

The life cycle may be divided into four main periods: *childhood and youth, early maturity, middle maturity,* and *later maturity.* Each of the stages has its distinctive function in the life of the individual. *Childhood and youth* are the time of the preparation for adult life and its responsibilities. *Early maturity* is the period of achievement in establishing the family, rearing children, and beginning an occupation. *Middle maturity* is concerned with the appraisal and re-orientation of life. *Later maturity* ideally affords the opportunity for a new freedom and fulfillment.

Among other points they can now decide is what organizations will best promote their interests and foster their creative powers. The choices can be lined up much as follows:

INTEREST	ORGANIZATION
Health and physical fitness	Sports and games clubs
Economic benefits	Lodges and remunerative hobbies
Intimate human associations	Golf, bowling, and other social activity clubs
Education	Adult education courses, discussion groups, lectures, conferences
Creative expression	Painting, music, ceramics, writing, and clubs
Service to the community	Civic action and welfare societies
Religion and ethics	Church activities, YM and YWCA, and other character-building agencies.

Burgess has undoubtedly provided us with an excellent general approach to a practical reorientation. In the main he meets the two criteria of greatest importance—*social utility* and *personal satisfaction.* It is our suspicion, however, that our self-actualizing group will reach this stage later than the population generality and will continue, as they have done in building their life-styles over a long period of years, to follow relatively unique directions. In their turtle shells of the half generation to either side of their chronological ages, they will continue to hold the comparative positions on the patterns of personality dimensions which set them apart as early as the first decade of becoming. The evidence from sources cited—

Terman, Terman and Oden, Maslow, Roe, Super, and Lehman—appears to support these assumptions.

A second relevant statement is that of Max Kaplan (1960, 409):

What are the needs of older persons? At least four approaches are available to us: (a) we can ask older persons themselves; (b) we can objectively study persons who are "successful" as older persons; (c) we can examine older persons who were not living successfully until certain therapies or measures were put into the situation and improvement resulted; and, finally, (d) we can attempt a synthesis of all the conclusions from the above. The last possibility will be examined briefly. The Institute of Gerontology of the State University of Iowa lists the following "needs and drives" of the older person in relation to leisure programs, based on the thinking of Clark Tibbetts:

a) Need to render some socially useful service
b) Need to be considered a part of the community
c) Need to occupy their increased leisure time in satisfying ways
d) Need to enjoy normal companionships
e) Need for recognition as an individual
f) Need for opportunity for self-expression and a sense of achievement
g) Need for health protection and care
h) Need for suitable mental stimulation
i) Need for suitable living arrangements and family relationships
j) Need for spiritual satisfaction

Some Special Considerations

Statements for the generalization of the forty-sixty decades do not apply with full force, in their specifics, for the self-actualizing group. This is very clear when we compare the statements of Crook and Heinstein (1958) regarding semiskilled and skilled production workers with those of Terman and Oden (1959) and Roe (1956) concerning populations where the efficiency variables are at an unusually high level. The major differences are in the life-styles, the kinds of occupational and avocational outlets, and the release from Maslow's (1954) lower-level needs at an earlier age.

In the matter of life-style there is no need to make more than a brief statement. From Chapter 3 we select a few of the indicators of self-actualization to make the point. Mature, well endowed and nurtured individuals, with a wide range of autonomous interests, an unusual multipotential for a variety of outlets in the culture, a generally high level of self- or formal education, creativeness, and self-sufficiency would not be such if their life-styles were as limited and circumscribed as those of many of the generality of the culture. From this group we expect leadership in many directions, and without their disproportionate contributions to the social structure, life in many of its dimensions would be the poorer for all of us. The Western culture, while giving women great freedom for self-expression compared with Eastern or African societies, places limitations compared with exploratory and manipulative opportunities of the male. Nevertheless, the life-styles of the self-actualizing women are as strikingly different from those of our population generality as is true of the men.

We find that occupationally our self-actualizers concentrate in the professional and creative areas. Medicine, the law, science, inventing, letters, music, the fine arts, and politics provide longer working lives and a wealth of alternatives when the time arrives to taper off and eventually retire. For example, the physician need not retire at a given age and date. By joining a clinic group, or finding a younger colleague to share a practice, our physicians can cut down on the time and energy demands while filling out their limited workdays with socially useful and personally satisfying functions. The lawyer can shape his late reaping years in the same way with the added opportunities which legal practice affords in judicial and political arenas. Scientists, frequently with college and university affiliations, have much the same pattern for an extended period in their specialties. The fine arts and music, barring certain limiting physical conditions related to vision, hearing, and fine eye-hand and eye-hand-tool coordinations, permit long continued part-time vocational efforts. As Super (1940) has indicated, vocations and avocations blend into each other well in these fields. Writers in certain fields may continue sowing and reach their peaks during these decades or even later.

Our self-actualizers include some men and women who value highly, and achieve, both power and wealth. Despite the fact that as members of the middle class, they contribute more than their share of the tax burden, it is for other reasons that our group usually fails to become "malefactors of great wealth." As has been stated above, they appear to meet the needs for adequate food, shelter, and other necessary and desirable surrounds quite early. In a number of manners they acquire educational opportunities and make use of them beyond generality. The majority appear to obtain this education in formal settings, but in the fine arts, writing, inventing, and music, degrees, particularly earned graduate degrees, do not seem crucial to self-actualization. When the contributions are in the management areas of business and industry, the financial rewards are higher, but job and financial security may be somewhat less, and for some the anxiety levels may be higher.

One group which contains its share of self-actualizers, but in which the life-style and vocational functions differ markedly in some ways from our others, is that of the military. Because this group will receive special attention later in the chapter, it is noted here only for emphasis. The warrant officers, chief petty officers, and officers of the armed forces in many instances meet the indicators of self-actualization listed in Chapter 3.

In summary to this point, our self-actualizers do not conform to the life-styles and behavior patterns of those with fewer responsibilities—and gifts. They are more free from the clock and calendars which govern so many. Time tends to be their ally and friend for a much longer period. Preparation for being older, and having been, is more a matter of a gradual change of direction for energy output than an easily charted decline. In short, qualitatively and quantitatively their life programs in the last half of living are as different from the general population norms as was true of the first half. Inasmuch as there is evidence of lack of information, lack of desirable skills for new directions, and some concern with choice-anxiety, which depends in varying degrees on the lack of information and skills, there will be, for some, a degree of lack of assurance. These matters are considered in greater detail in Chapters 8 and 9. We now give our attention to special subgroups among the self-actualizing—women, members of the military, and certain smaller, but important sub-subgroups including those who change directions markedly in the periods of sowing and early reaping.

BEING—REAPING

THE LADIES AND OTHERS

In Chapter 3, Terman and Oden (1959, 145) were quoted regarding the accomplishments of the women in their group despite the large proportion of them who had devoted their lives to being homemakers. Because our next consideration also is so well said by Terman and Oden, we continue the earlier quotation:

> Our gifted women, in the main, however, are housewives, and many who also work outside the home do so more to relieve the monotony of household duties or to supplement the family income rather than through a desire for a serious career. There are many intangible kinds of accomplishment and success open to the housewife, and it is debatable whether the fact that a majority of gifted women prefer housewifery to more intellectual pursuits represents a net waste of brainpower. Although it is possible by means of rating scales to measure with fair accuracy the achievement of a scientist or a professional or business man, no one has yet devised a way to measure the contribution of a woman who makes her marriage a success, inspires her husband, and sends forth well-trained children into the world.

It would be difficult to improve on the quotation above, but it does not carry us far enough into the future. Environmental, cultural mold traits unquestionably contribute strong forces to buttress the biological drives which place the female in the roles of housewifery. But there are also the effects of culturally traumatic periods which involve heavy stress on many individuals related to some extent to Murray's *press* and Sullivan's *crisis stamping* concepts and constructs. Terman's group could be labeled "teen-agers of the Great Depression." The half generation behind them, in a like manner, might be called "adolescents of World War II." One can know only vaguely the impact of these events in the shaping of specific personality dimensions or the global result, but it seems that there must be shaping by the second dynamic when the personality structure is still quite flexible.

In dealing with individuals who learned and overlearned some important roles and coping behavior thirty to forty years ago, one must be most cautious in applying the norms of the present. If Cattell's "first law of motion" for psychology—resistance to change —is operative, the need for caution is even more emphasized. This is not to deny flexibility and the possibility of shifting value weights and even some vectors of a stable personality at any age, but we are not well supplied with meaningful data of a normative kind in these areas of personality dimensions about the self-actualizing group between the ages of forty and sixty. In fact, we are not even in agreement as to the names for the crucial dimensions.

Terman's early life was in an America much different in its mores, morals, and philosophy than the America of today. His 1925 eleven-year-olds must be judged in part with the half generation—the one- to twenty-five-year-olds at that time—relative to their cultural turtle shells. His group differs from present day eleven-year-olds, for example, in the average level of expected formal education; the degree to which real responsibilities were not only available to, but were forced on, teen-agers; the impact of child labor laws; the years of life expectancy; the position and images of the married woman; the number and quality of openings for able women to self-actualize; and the shift from a still quite rural, agricultural, frontier-minded aura to that of a highly complex, urban living philosophy. Thus, in considering the sample, we must give attention to Terman and his group in the light of the surrounds, environments, and fields in which their personalities and perceptions were most shaped and programmed. These considerations handicap us somewhat both in research and professional practice.

Whether or not we should encourage filling time with personally satisfying, but socially nonproductive, activities is, as Terman states in the quotation above, a debatable question. That self-actualizing women between forty-five and sixty-five do constitute a formidable pool of social assets does not appear so debatable. The basal questions concern what they want to do with their time and gifts. Few politicians are brave enough to attempt regimentation in this regard! If we assume that all or most of these individuals have a quite clear understanding of personal, environmental, and interaction dynamics, personal decisions and behaviors will tend to be optimal for each such individual. If, on the other hand, we assume that many lack information, skills, assurance, and the general ability to make sure, reality-oriented decisions, then it seems to be a legitimate interest to investigate ways and means for providing these lacks when the services are sought by clients. This is even more important if we assume further that added knowledge of such ways and means will result in different, and more personally satisfying and socially useful, decisions and behaviors. If we hold to our first assumption, self-contained optimal decision making, the battle is over. What our lady prefers to do is the best she can do. If we make the second assumption, that some elements for optimal decision making are lacking, then the ways and means for learning how to remedy possible lacks become important for those who wish remedies. No one is known to the author wise enough to "teach" the remedies. There are some, perhaps, who can help the individual *to learn* with greater facility through the provision of a structure for studying the three dynamics.

However, the major concern here is with the newly gained freedom of the wife and mother who now faces the difficult task of adapting and adjusting to a family unit of two. In the paragraphs above she has been considered as a possible national resource for goods and/or services. Her own personal time-using desires now take over. Here too, there are problems for some. The self-images will tend to shift. The images which surround protecting and caring for children are no longer realistic under most circumstances, although one may maintain part of this image with grandchildren, present or prospective. The chores of being a Den Mother, chauffeur, cook, laundress, and caterer social hostess for teen-agers have dropped out and left time to be filled. Statuses have changed. The younger parent friends who shared youth activities and the related social endeavors may drop from the scheme of things. Instead of being a senior member and consultant of this group, one becomes a junior member of a group somewhat older. The memberships in some more or less formal club groups lapse, and the self-expression and belongingness which they provided must now be dropped or supplied in other groups. It is fortunate that so many of the self-actualizers, even though concentrated effort may not have been possible for a long time, have personal resources on which they can be capitalizing. She has put one career behind her. As Terman said, she has "made her marriage a success, inspired her husband, and sent forth well-trained children into the world."

In the new freedom there is still responsibility to maintain the marriage, albeit under different circumstances and with different goals and values. There is also the continuing inspiration for her husband who has fifteen, twenty, or more, career years remaining. These responsibilities will tend to take less time and attention than was true in the years of sowing and early reaping. For purposes of easier communication, let us categorize the conditions which different subgroups of our self-actualizing women face. These are (1) intact careers, (2) intact avocations, (3) suspended careers and avocations, and (4) the opportunity to follow coinciding interests, aptitudes, achievements, and abilities. In the following chapter thumbnail case histories are presented which illustrate each category.

Women with Intact Careers

It is not unusual for career women to marry career men. In some instances the marriage takes place after both careers are launched. Thus physicians marry physicians, lawyers marry lawyers, musicians marry musicians, and teachers marry teachers. It is obvious too that cross-fertilization takes place, i.e., physicians marry musicians, accountants marry teachers, and writers marry inventors. In other circumstances the one already launched provides the means for the other to complete education and training. In still others, for example, premedics marry premedics. The net result is a professional worker who keeps her hand in while she makes her chief vocation that of homemaker. When the freedom of the middle years becomes a reality, the wife invests the time formerly taken by the family in the career and becomes a full-time, successful, professional practitioner. For these women the march of time is not especially disturbing.

Women with Intact Avocations

In this category one is likely to encounter many of those with interests and achievements in writing and the fine arts. The individual has kept in limited practice when time and the mood permitted. Music, painting, sculpture, ceramics, short stories, novels, and motion picture and television scripts will be found among the achievements. Sometimes the avocation is a quasi vocation with an appreciable income and few formal obligations. Often the activity is for its own sake and the personal satisfaction of the activity. Within this category many of our self-actualizers find the new freedom and time assets in expanding the life space and avoiding the constrictions which limit so many others. Organizers and managers move into the exciting scramble of politics; others join state, regional, and national social club activities or movements for doing or saving something; and still others devote time to teaching bridge and achieving the expert class. In fact, for many of our women the very number of realistic intriguing possibilities creates problems.

Suspended Careers and Avocations

A number of years ago, when Henry Ford was beginning to change America, there was an annual pilgrimage to the railway station to watch the new lady teachers arrive. In the Middle West and West there was a shortage of wives and prospective wives. As one local wit put it, "Them with two heads is usually second choice." This was an excellent example of the suspended career. Teaching not only was one of the quickest ways to a professional career into which young ladies were encouraged to enter, but it had also many of the characteristics of a hunting license.

Times have changed. The careers for women (and the hunting prerogatives) have shifted markedly to college and university campuses. However, the suspension of careers is still a usual happening. For example, nurses, social workers, chemists, mathematicians, programmers, teachers, physical and occupational therapists, medical and dental technicians, and private secretaries are all subject to suspended careers after a relatively short working period. During the twenty to thirty years when homemaking is the career, the original skills are diminished through disuse. When the middle years provide new freedom and time begins to hang heavy, the old skills are considered as possibilities for refurbishing.

In this category there are problems. One concerns the status of the individual. The vocational and avocational skills which were deemed appropriate for a young woman in the stage of becoming may now be frowned upon by the social groups to which she belongs. Or they may not be considered by the family as in keeping with the husband's occupational status. Or automation and electronics may have caused obsolescence. Images have changed. New developments, technical and professional, require somewhat lengthy personal "retooling" for reentry into the field. With the change in self-images, there may be lack of assurance regarding competencies in even mildly competitive enterprises. There may be a serious lack of information as to how and where one goes about regaining old skills and creating new ones. The true self-actualizer will tend to make adequate adaptations and adjustments; borderliners may need greater help. Physicians, psychiatrists, and psychologists in private practice and on the campuses of educational institutions meet both types constantly. If there are financial and other responsibilities, the urgency of the seeking for help may approach desperation.

Those Who Follow Coinciding Interests, Achievements, Aptitudes, and Abilities

Our largest subgroup is that which falls into none of the categories already examined. The creativity, self-sufficiency, leadership, and other characteristics of self-actualizing individuals have been invested in the family with all the desirable outcomes to which Terman referred. These outcomes emphasize intangibles which are of so much importance in living and life. They are elusive because they are so subtly woven into the web of social living at the deep sentiment-value level of the family. Nor are these achievements easily marketed in our society by an able woman with a strong need and desire to expand, explore, practice social manipulation, and avoid the constrictions she sees occurring in so many around her.

The history of individuals in this category is one of "no place to go." When physicians write their memoirs of practice, usually we find somewhere in the pages references to "neurotic, middle-aged women." Because the older stereotypes of the physician in general practice included the role of family confessor as well as that of a father surrogate, it is not surprising that many self-actualizing women turned to the perceived best source of help. Because psychiatric services have become more available and better understood, it is probable that these women are increasingly numbered among their patients. This is also true for the adjustment psychologist in private practice. However, since many of these individuals face a major problem of *adaptation,* even though there are always loadings of *adjustment,* one may suspect that attention focused chiefly on internalized problems of psychological equilibrium is not a total answer. It seems only fair to comment that, by and large, our group still has "not many places to go." The professional facilitation of people matching themselves to nonvocational situations and environments is a social need that is not being fully met. Even though interests, achievements, aptitudes and abilities indicate desirable directions for a person, they are of little use if the possessor does not recognize the patterns and directions and can find no one who is qualified to help banish some of the lack of information and assurance.

We meet the ladies again in the following chapter. The previously mentioned thumbnail case histories will be used to illustrate the presentations above. We focus attention now on another subgroup, self-actualizers leaving the military services for civilian life.

GENTLEMEN AND LADIES IN UNIFORM

During times of peace, however uneasy, the military organizations are not well known or understood by most of us. Unless one has had opportunities to work closely with military personnel, there is a lack of appreciation for the talents so many of them possess. One can, of course, point to the impressive numbers who have been President of the United States, senators, representatives, college and university presidents, leaders in business and industry, writers, and inventors. What is more important here is that each such person left one career, after the period of sowing, and entered a new one often unrelated to the specifics of personal military functions. Many reached mountain peaks of some altitude in the military service, "retired," and promptly charged to the tops of higher and different mountains.

This group of self-actualizers has careers which are subject to conditions different from most civilian pursuits. After twenty, twenty-five, or thirty years, they can retire. While this is true in other walks of life, military men and women frequently reach twenty years of service while still in the late thirties or early forties. Even those with much brass on the shoulders begin to leave the service in the forty-five to fifty-five decade. Thus, with retirement pay which provides bread and butter, those who are impelled to climb more mountains are in an excellent position for selecting appropriate ranges. The writer cannot find sufficient data from which to make an analysis of any great value. It is possible to hypothesize categories such as: (1) general administrative skills with application in business and industry as well as higher education; (2) high-level professional and technical skills related to engineering and various branches of electronics such as communications and data processing; (3) specialties related to curricular offerings in secondary and higher education, such as mathematics and language, or, for a few, experiences which give them an unusual grasp of geography and political science; (4) demonstrated skills in human relations which open careers in politics and social service promotional endeavors; (5) miscellaneous experiences which lead into sales, private business enterprises, and community leadership other than politics.

Schools of education have been alert to this excellent pool of teaching and administrative material. Again without research for validation, it is the author's impression that an impressive number of ex-warrant officers, petty officers, and just plain officers are to be found in our secondary schools, junior colleges, and colleges as teachers and administrators. We are aware from the newspaper stories of those who enter business and industry in higher managerial echelons or who become college or university presidents. We know very little about those who are self-actualizing below the headline level.

The issue of importance to us here is that of how they make their plans and choose their mountains. Even when one has been out of touch with military personnel for a long period of time, the steady mail and requests for appointments indicate that they need help. A cruise on a battle wagon a few years ago by the writer turned into an experience of consulting with individuals regarding second-career planning. An exchange of views with colleagues showed a similar awareness of this group's need for help when faced with problems of *adapting* to civilian life. In one respect they resemble our ladies; they have no clearly indicated place to go for professional aid.

Recapitulating, here is a self-actualizing group with socially important aptitudes, abilities, and achievements. There is need by many to translate these assets from a military to a civilian setting. The translation is not always a one-to-one relationship between military functions and civilian outlets. There appears to be a need for psychologists who specialize in the distributive aspects of adaptation with mature, normal, self-actualizing clients. The reader will meet some of these military self-actualizers as disguised cases in the next chapter.

THOSE WHO ARE NEITHER LADIES NOR RETIRED FROM THE MILITARY

In numbers, those who are not ladies or retired from the military are our largest group. But they differ so much in their individual personality patterns, perceptions, and reality testing that they defy neat ordering. Included are those from business and industry who, for a variety of reasons, wish a change of scenery which permits challenging activity other than that in which they have already sowed. We have also the thoughtful person who wishes to plan some distance ahead in order to taper off from legal or medical practice. Then there are those who have inherited money and wish to serve humanity; those who can now see a way to realize dreams of an earlier period without having to depend on the vicarious satisfactions which arise from coercing the children into living someone else's dreams; those who are curious and wish to explore themselves a bit more intensively; and those who just don't have anything else to occupy their time and wish someone of perceived professional status as a listener.

To classify this diversity is perceived by the writer as too difficult a task. As a substitute for this kind of dividing of souls, a brief consideration is given below to quite common problem conditions and situations. These we name *heads against the ceiling, professional traps,* and *multipotentiality.* All of these conditions can conceivably affect the same person at the same time. However, it is necessary for purposes of communication to deal with them one at a time.

Heads Against the Ceiling

The American dream of log cabin to White House still persists. Horatio Alger, Progressive Education, permissiveness, and the 1947–1957 decade for the "everyone adjusting everyone crusade" all contributed to changes in our perceptions of the dream. We developed a belief that the march from the log cabin to our destinations was "by the numbers." We entered the first grade. Each year we were promoted. (It was the teacher's fault if we failed. "Children don't fail—just teachers.") We marched through grades one to twelve. Our personalities were protected by avoiding comparative grading systems. This might damage the high achiever, but he or she was probably antisocial. High school was more of the same.

Colleges and universities were not so pliable, but even in these strongholds of reactionary practices, we taught fly tying and picnic cookery. If one did not choose to go to college, the march through promotions to the career top was popularly considered more of the same. Then there was Sputnik. Things haven't been the same since —there comes a time to awaken from the finest dream.

For the period of sowing, the rungs of our ladder lead us ever upward. But sooner or later, usually between the fortieth and sixtieth birthdays, our personal ladder ends at a ceiling. The realization strikes home that the probability for appreciable advancement is remote. Income is also approaching its peak. Younger men and women move by us in the status hierarchy. This moment of truth is for some a prelude to helpful psychotherapy. Others quietly handle the adjustment and adaptation problems themselves. Still others butt their heads against the ceiling in an attempt to break through. And there are those who shift to a ladder under a higher ceiling. The ceiling is encountered relatively early by some and at an amazingly late time by others, but for all of us the ladder eventually ends at a ceiling. It is a stressful period for most men and women, including our self-actualizers. But the manner of personal handling is a test of whether or not the crucial dimensions of self-actualization still exist in the person.

It is possible that the phenomenon is more prevalent in business careers than in others. It seems that the more competitive the endeavor is, the more drastic the results of the situation will be in terms of undermining goals and values and forcing changes in attitudinal and sentiment loadings on the individual. The results involve our *roles* for external, overt behavior and our *masks* for internalized, covert behavior. Regardless of what competent source of professional help is sought, it seems that this is a period in which it can be most useful. Darley and Hagenah (1955, 13–14) go to the heart of our ladder and ceiling problem when they say:

It is of some slight relevance that our popular literature today often deals with the period of doubt in men's careers, in the decade of their forties. The early and often costly years of training are out of the way; marriage and the raising of children—hostages to fortune—are well along; success and material well-being beyond the subsistence level are established. The pressure eases enough to permit some introspection, some stock-taking. If doubt is to supervene, this is the time. Has the trap closed forever? Do the years to come hold advancement and material success? Has the last chance to change or progress gone by? Do these daily tasks hold the meaning and satisfaction they once held? Has the point of no return been reached?

Professional Traps

The terminology is from Darley and Hagenah (1955, 12–16). The concern is with men and women who commit themselves to lengthy and expensive preparation for a career during the later years of becoming. Examples of the occupational titles are those found on the scales of the Strong Vocational Interest Blank. The young chemist, accountant, teacher, administrator, engineer, or any one of a large number of other labels enters the field in which he has prepared. He, or she, is successful in terms of the indicators of success—promotions, increasing income, membership in status organizations, publications, home ownership—and appears busy and happy throughout the period of sowing. And then the trap is sprung.

An oversimplification of the situation is to describe it as a matter of a high level of potentiality in the efficiency variables without sufficient attention to other noncongruent personality dimensions and patterns. The needs, wants, goals, values, and other components of motivation, learning, and perception in the unique individual have not been given appropriate weighting in long-circuited choice making. In Chapter 2 interests were briefly discussed. The hypothesis was advanced that interests may be crucial in focusing the need, want, goal, and value system for adaptation to the Western environment. Although no one instrument, or known collection of psychometric devices, can give us *complete* men or women or even complete hypothetical men and women, the writer is still impressed with the diagnostic and assessment value of the Strong blank in qualified professional hands. Confining this statement to the vocational area, if the career occupations run counter to the patterns of the individual on the Strong profile, one seems sometimes to find serious problems of the type we are discussing, far beyond chance expectancy (see Sarbin and Anderson, 1942).

We return to our client who, at forty-two, finds that he doesn't like being a certified public accountant, or rather, doing what certified public accountants do and associating with them constantly. Darley and Hagenah (1955, 15–16) offer five possible outcomes to which the writer adds a sixth. The alternatives are (1) develop socially acceptable and compensatory hobbies; (2) develop personality and behavioral conflicts at home and/or on the job; (3) redefine job components to more closely approximate personal interest patterns; (4) establish a poor performance record (with either conscious or unconscious motivation) and escape through discharge; and (5) escape the trap during social upheavals, such as a war or major depression. It is of interest to note the Darley-Hagenah illustrations of this last point (15–16):

> Other examples of the impact of social forces can be found, and might serve to illuminate some of our problems of jobs and interests if appropriate research and case studies could be made.
>
> Such an illustration would emerge if we studied the effect of a concentrated and heavily subsidized drive to attract men and women to certain kinds of professional fields. At the end of the war, both psychiatrists and clinical psychologists were judged to be in short supply, and the Veterans Administration and the United States Public Health Service poured substantial funds into training programs for these fields. Did this campaign bring to the professions a different group of people than might have come under less external and financial pressure? In this instance, a trap was laid, to continue our figure of speech, and it is important to consider the kind of people that were caught. What of their abilities, their motivations, their interests, and their satisfactions in the task components of the job title they ultimately came to bear?

Our sixth outcome, or alternative, is one taken by a few choice souls among our self-actualizers who—despite hurdles, including age—change careers. Super and Crites (1962) present the major facets of measured and estimated career interests, their origin, and possible directions. Change of career may involve a real and drastic change, for example, from engineer to psychotherapist. There are many individuals who have obtained the M.D. degree and, after successful medical practice, also have earned the Ph.D. degree in psychology. Others have reversed the process moving from the Ph.D. degree to the M.D. Lawyers become accountants and accountants lawyers, in the forty-fifty or even the fifty-sixty decades. Dentists and veterinarians have been known to practice successfully and then become physicians. It is not unusual for women to prepare for an administrative career by becoming graduate nurses with a college degree, or degrees. These people do not escape the trap—they ignore it. We have here a parallel to the old concept of the "blind alley" job. As Hahn and MacLean (1955) said, "There are no blind alley jobs; only blind alley people."

However, the drastic career switch is not usually necessary because in so many of the professions and higher administrative positions in business and industry and government there is great freedom for intralabel mobility. Lawyers are a particularly good example of this. There is not only opportunity to shift among and between specialties within the legal framework, there is also politics, business administration, and governmental specialization at all levels. Some of these intralaw shifts may be at least as great as the differences between law and other seemingly discrete occupational labels such as certified public accountant. This flexibility and mobility within a label is also characteristic of medicine. In many states general practitioners are permitted to practice psychiatry if they so desire. Major changes in the medical armamentarium, such as the use of antibiotics, may alter greatly a specialty such as eye-ear-nose-and-throat. When these changes occur because of technological or scientific discoveries, the mobility of the practitioners becomes evident as they shift to other areas of medical practice.

What has been said above is not intended to brush away the reality of an individual being trapped. As can be seen in the case of Mr. C-1 in Chapter 5, the trap is evident. It is true that even the most able person can have such difficulties because of events beyond his control. But being trapped often can stem from lack of information, lack of skill, or lack of assurance. Self-actualizers, by definition, have personal resources which permit them to avoid or escape from traps.

Multipotentiality

Multipotentiality of direction and depth in social behaviors has been introduced into previous paragraphs while considering vocational and avocational interests. However, the multipotentialities of many self-actualizing individuals is amazing even to those who have dealt with many such. The reader who wishes more information and discussion on this matter will do well to consult *Identity and anxiety* (Stein, Viditch, and White, 1960); *Human potentialities* (Gardner Murphy, 1958); and *Personality and social encounter* (Gordon Allport, 1960). Hahn and MacLean (1955) speak of multipotentiality as follows:

Occupational multipotentiality creates further complexities in the solution of educational-vocational problems. As has been suggested, any occupational field affords a large number of related patterns of work at various levels. Roughly speaking, the 10 per cent of the population that is most gifted in scholastic abilities becomes the professional and executive group of gainfully employed workers if they do not fail for these same reasons to get work at their proper level. While such individuals who possess enough ability and training to belong to this group will tend to win their way into jobs at a level commensurate with their abilities, counselors know that they usually are competent to perform the functions of hundreds of lower level jobs in the field. For example, a naval admiral is usually skilled in ship operations, navigation, aiming and firing weapons, scrubbing decks, etc., but does none of them, and a college president may know how to teach biology or to operate the heating plant. Some of these individuals with high level abilities prefer to earn their livelihoods at levels well below their potentialities. The authors have known a number of these. They often quite ably work out a life pattern for themselves in which their jobs serve only as a financial base for support and neither consume much time nor demand strenuous effort. Instead they pour their time and energy into devotion to happy family life, voluntary public service, and pleasant so-called "leisure time" activities such as music, art, gardening, and the like. While such patterns of behavior are contrary to our general cultural mores, there appear to be a growing number of persons in our society who adopt them. This may well be evidence of a trend in our society as steam, electric, and atomic power replace muscle power in both productive and service occupations.

In a sense, the discussion of multipotentiality overlaps that of professional traps. It seems probable that few of us realize how many social or socially oriented behaviors are possible for us. As has been stated, the self-actualizer is more aware of this situation than his more prosaic fellows. For the group which has relatively unstructured, but high level aptitudes, abilities, and interests, it is in this condition of multipotentiality that new directions may be found.

IN SUMMARY

This chapter has been a too brief overview of the self-actualizing client. A group of author-selected dimensions of self-actualization has been presented. The loss of perceived utility and joy in our overlearned career skills of the sowing and early reaping decades have been considered. The shift from personal and career establishment to a stable maintenance plateau has had a place. We have journeyed through the rationale for planning the second half of life and considered general ways and means for such planning. Certain differences in the life-styles and patterns of men and women received attention. The relatively unique situations of those who have followed a military-first career have been presented and briefly discussed. Certain special considerations centering about ladders and ceilings, professional traps, and multipotentiality filled a few pages. We have arrived now at the point where it may be logical to answer the demand of the man from Missouri—"Show me one!" In the next chapter our chief consideration will be brief, illustrative case summaries to highlight the materials in this chapter.

Chapter 5

PEOPLE

IN THE PRECEDING chapter attention was directed to categories of clients and the general situations which individuals in these categories faced in adapting and adjusting to the reaping period of being. In order to focus these generalizations more sharply, this chapter is devoted to thumbnail case histories of clients. The cases are based on actual people, but the ethical necessity for disguising identities forces liberties with some of the data. However, the essentials are not distorted to a point where the cases are fabrications. Names, locations, and some time sequences have been altered as have the sizes of families. The ages are accurate at the time the professional relationship existed.

Each case history is accompanied by judgments regarding the dimensions of self-actualization and compares the psychologist-inferred evaluation with the client self-images and concepts. These judgments are, of course, clinically derived, thus lacking any demonstrable validity or reliability. What the validity and reliability of the author's clinical judgments are is indeed dealing with unknown parameters. Each case history also includes the sex, age, formal education, and marital status of the client. For most of the cases, a brief follow-up is included.

The dimensions used to describe and identify those who are labeled self-actualizing were discussed in the preceding chapter. They are vague and poorly defined. However, despite our lack of sound research which might permit greater clarity, five years of attention with colleagues and graduate students leads to the belief that there is meaningful communication when the terms are used. Only one dimension, *efficiency variables,* can be entered with confidence from the research. Even with this rubric, the evaluation for the cases is inferred. It is most difficult to find psychometric devices suitable for the population about which this book is written.

There was no referral to psychotherapists because of unusual problems of adjustment in any of the histories cited. As internalized, covert feelings and emotions are always present in the normal individual; this is not a denial that the professional relationship involved adjustment loadings. It was, however, the opinion of the writer that in all instances the individual had the personal resources to deal with these adjustment difficulties without a strong need for professional attention to them.

Figure 1 is presented as a convenient summary form with which the reader can review the dimensions of self-actualization used in this book, specifically in Chapter 3 where self-actualization is more fully discussed. This form and modifications of it have been useful in communicating with clients and colleagues.

We turn now to the representative case summaries. The reader will note that none of the individuals presented appear to fall at the level of the Maslow (1954) sample. A number of them would have been included in a sample comparable to that of Terman (1926). Probably such individuals will be encountered about seven to ten times in one hundred of the general population.

THE LADIES

Four of the ladies are included in this section. Three of them completed a formal four-year college degree program. One had a graduate degree at the time the professional relationship existed. A second one completed a professional two-year certification program subsequent to the psychoevaluation. The fourth completed high school in an academic curriculum and spent two years in obtaining professional certification supplemented by nondegree professional training at various times.

Three were married and mothers. One never married. None could be called wealthy or particularly privileged. Three were definitely middle and upper-middle class in their family background. The fourth was from a distinguished professional family. One was the daughter of an immigrant. All were bored with much that they did most of the time from about the age of forty. In fact, *taedium vitae* was marked in all of the cases presented in this chapter. With this as introduction we turn now to Mrs. A-1.

Mrs. A-1

Age 46; married; 3 children; 16 years of formal education

Evaluation: lack of information; no intact career or avocational resources; coinciding interests, achievements, aptitudes, and abilities; minimum IQ equivalent 125

The client was married to a well-established professional man. There were three children, two girls and a boy. The youngest, a daughter, was seventeen. The elder girl was married with one child. The son was a premedical student in a major private university. Mrs. A-1 was attractive, well groomed, and reflected her educational backgrounds. The four walls of a home could no longer contain her. She played good bridge, as did her husband. No hobbies, as she had invested her time wholeheartedly in raising her family and meeting the social obligations which her husband's professional status demanded.

Figure 1 Dimensions of Self-actualization

Client*____________________________________*M. F.

***Mar.*____*Single*____*Div.*____*Widow*____*Age*____**

***Widower*____**

Efficiency variables	***(1)***	
Self-expression, independence, vocational satisfaction	***(2)***	
Leadership	***(3)***	
Performance vs. potential	***(4)***	
Social-political	***(5)***	
Social contribution	***(6)***	
Self-sufficiency	***(7)***	
Creativity	***(8)***	
Maturity	***(9)***	
Social-vocational multipotentiality	***(10)***	

(1) problem solving at complex levels; formal education and/or equivalents; performance products of problem solving: ***(2) life-style which is distinctive,*** reality tested noncomformance, career selection and growth consonant with personality dimensions: ***(3) is looked up to and followed*** by others in areas of competence: ***(4)*** the degree to which ***demonstrated achievement is correlated with estimated peak performance: (5) avoidance of extremes*** which interfere with social relationships and personal expansion: **(6)** ***impact on subcultures*** and culture in promoting and advancing the social good: **(7)** ***ability to make decisions*** and carry through to effective results without great dependence on others for support: ***(8) demonstrated performance in creating novel solutions*** to complex problems; arrangement of matter in new or different forms; development and

Self-estimates ____________

Peer estimates ____________

Professional estimates ________

General population average	***75th percentile general population***	***90th percentile***

expansion of ideas through words, expressive behavior, or art forms—graphic or temporal: *(9)* demonstrated possession of autonomous interests, self-objectivity, and an integrated and unified philosophy of life: ***(10) demonstrated ability to perform in several areas*** of the life pattern at a high level; achievement of outstanding performance in several facets of a major career area; competence in generalizing from one area of special competence to related areas; ability to shift from one effort to another without appreciable loss of speed or power of performance; demonstrated achievement in such seemingly diverse fields as professional and/or technical efforts, organization and administration, community planning, long-circuited programs over months and years, in more than one important aspect of social living.

The client appeared to have status needs for herself as a person. Her self-actualization profile indicates that she underestimated her own potentials for developing a second career. Only in the matter of self-sufficiency did her self-concepts match closely the psychologist's estimates. Mrs. A-1 was not well informed as to ways and means by which she might use her potentials for a second vocation or avocation. She had considered a number of possibilities including voluntary services to hospitals, political activities as an office helper, and service work with the girl scouts. She had given her services to a hospital for a period of six months but did not find that what she did was important to her or provided a satisfactory outlet for her unrest and needs for self-actualization. She rated herself on the dimensions of self-actualization against women in general as follows:

Self-actualizing dimensions	*Self-rating, percentile*	*Psychologist rating, percentile*
Efficiency variables	65	90
Self-expression	50	90
Leadership	70	80
Performance vs. potential	60	80
Social-political	70	80
Social contributions	55	75
Self-sufficiency	75	90
Creativity	50	70
Maturity	65	90
Social-vocational multipotentiality	65	90

Given a list of descriptive terms she characterized herself by the traits and temperaments which are marked with an asterisk below. (Those which are boldface are the psychologist's judgments.)

excitable, depressed, **sociable,*** sense of humor,* **hard working,*** shy, love of excitement, **conscientious,*** **ambitious,** dreamer, happy, **worried,*** confident,* **reserved,** spontaneous,* nervous, **capable, leader, calm,*** **persevering,*** **controlled,*** sensitive, **hate regulations, independent,*** lack self-confidence,* irritable,* **patient, tolerant**

Mrs. A-1 completed the Strong Vocational Interest Blank for men. She showed no interests in groups I, II, III, IV, VI, VII, X, and XI. A primary pattern emerged in group V—social welfare. In group IX an A was recorded on the Life Insurance Salesman scale. Interest Maturity was half a standard deviation above the mean, as was Occupational Level. The M-F scale was average. Mrs. A-1 made her decisions and so announced in the third, and last, interview. She entered a professional training program, persisted for two years, and earned an M.S. degree and a state certificate. Mrs. A-1 worked full time for a short period to gain experience and then made arrangements to work part time with a private agency. Five years after this beginning she was still busy, although her patterns of activity moved steadily in the direction of administrative functions. A follow-up indicated excellent family relationships, a somewhat greater social life, and much heavier participation in local politics than had earlier been the case. The younger daughter has completed college, is engaged, and is working in an advertising agency. The son is in medical school.

The Psychologist's Corner

Mrs. A-1, in terms of Pepinsky's categories, lacked information and was concerned with choice-anxiety. Potential skills of a high order were present. Lack of assurance was of no importance. The psychotherapy indicators were negative. The information which she wanted appears to have been confirmation of her own self-images and certain specifics concerning directions for her efforts which would permit her to meet the new goals for a second career in a reasonable period of time. With these informations supplied, she did what one would have expected, she moved in a straight line toward a clear objective. That she would have found reasonably satisfactory solutions for a new career without the help of a psychologist seems obvious. What she probably gained from professional consultation was a saving in time. At no point would the term *patient* have applied. There was no need to continue the relationship over a longer span of time or a greater number of interviews.

It is emphasized also that few aspects of vocational advisement were wanted by Mrs. A-1 or supplied by the psychologist. In fact, it is a distinct impression that an attempt to advise would have been strongly resisted. Some bibliocommunication was involved, including university catalogs, descriptive occupational information to a limited degree, and the psychologist's written report which was discussed informally some time after the third formal interview. One interview provided a bit of ventilation, but attention to problems of adjustment did not appear desired nor was there any attempt at psychotherapy on the part of the psychologist.

Mrs. A-1 is presented in these pages as an example of the self-actualizing woman who is closing out the career of motherhood without an intact vocation or avocation, or a suspended career, but who has coinciding interests, achievements, aptitudes, and abilities. Her second career as a professional worker has been successfully launched, and her third, as an administrator, is possible. There is a hearteningly large number of women like her, and they are important.

Mrs. A-2

Age 52; widow; 7 children; 14 years of formal education

Evaluation: lack of assurance, choice-anxiety, intact career, no psychotherapeutic indicators, minimum IQ equivalent 120

The client was the widow of a moderately successful business executive. The seven children, four boys and three girls, are outstanding tributes to the parents and their careers as mother and father. All the girls are married as are the boys. Among the children, there is no record of divorce. Six of the seven children have completed college educations. The boys are all engaged in business careers similar to that of the father.

Mrs. A-2 meets all of the criteria which Terman sets for the wife-mother career at a high level. This joint career extended over a period of thirty-two years before the youngest child achieved a driver's license. Because the original ancillary medical career was maintained throughout the mother-wife career span, the problem is one of fighting off the mother images of the children and making the choice of being what the children perceive the mother role to be, or of putting the intact or suspended career to use.

The discrepancies between the client and psychologist evaluations of self-actualizing dimensions are marked.

Self-actualizing dimensions	*Self-rating, percentile*	*Psychologist rating, percentile*
Efficiency variables	60	85
Self-expression	55	75
Leadership	45	65
Performance vs. potential	40	75
Social-political	65	85
Social contribution	60	90
Self-sufficiency	60	90
Creativity	55	60
Maturity	65	95
Social-vocational multipotentiality	55	90

Mrs. A-2 differed greatly from the psychologist in her selection of the traits she claimed were characteristic of her.

> excitable,* **depressed,*** **sociable,*** **sense of humor,*** **hard working,** shy,* **love excitement, conscientious,*** ambitious, dreamer, happy, **worried,*** confident, **reserved,*** spontaneous, nervous,* **capable, leader, calm, persevering, controlled, sensitive,*** hate regulations, **independent, lack self-confidence,*** irritable, **patient, tolerant***

Mrs. A-2 has been known to the writer for a long period of time as a family friend. Aside from the judgments made in interview situations regarding the dimensions of self-actualization and traits indicated above, there was no need or opportunity for the use of psychometric devices. The life-style appears clear from personal observations and discussions with the children and friends.

The present status of the client is still involved with lack of assurance and choice-anxiety. There has been no strong move either to reinstate career skills which are intact or to surrender completely to the family pressures.

The Psychologist's Corner

The conflict between roles, her own perceptions, and the perceptions of the children has not been resolved. Personal adjustment appears excellent despite the problems of adaptation. Financial difficulties are not present. One looks for indicators which would point to a referral for psychotherapy, but they refuse to appear. Perhaps the thirty years of one major role has made a shift most difficult, although there are career openings for her at an appropriate level. She perceives time as an increasingly greater enemy and will continue to do so until the role choice-anxiety is resolved. Her third career degrees of freedom are numerous.

Mrs. A-3

Age 44; married; 3 children; 18 years of formal education

Evaluation: methodical self-study and curiosity, no psychotherapeutic indicators, minimum IQ equivalent 135

The client was a chic, self-possessed, sophisticated, well-educated individual. The three children, all male, were twenty, nineteen, and seventeen years of age. The oldest was a college junior in a general liberal arts program. The second boy was a college freshman in a college of engineering. The youngest was about to graduate from high school and planned on college. The husband was a moderately successful writer on technical subjects for industrial publications with some editorial responsibilities for such publications.

Mrs. A-3 had completed the B.S. degree in physics and mathematics, taught in secondary schools for one year, married, and then went back to a university and completed the M.S. degree in mathematics. Her father was a physics professor in a large university, and her mother had completed a B.A. in the humanities. Mrs. A-3 worked with her husband helping to write where her mathematical background was of interest and use. Her self-actualizing dimensions as perceived by herself and the psychologist are as follows:

Self-actualizing dimensions	*Self-rating, percentile*	*Psychologist rating, percentile*
Efficiency variables	90	95
Self-expression	85	95
Leadership	90	60
Performance vs. potential	95	85
Social-political	95	85
Social contribution	90	80
Self-sufficiency	95	95
Creativity	90	80
Maturity	95	95
Social-vocational multipotentiality	85	95

Mrs. A-3 reflects psychologist opinion and observations closely when she characterizes herself by indicating terms which she believes apply to her.

> excitable, depressed, **sociable,*** **sense of humor,*** hard working, shy, love excitement,* **conscientious, ambitious,** dreamer, **happy,*** worried, **confident,*** **reserved,*** **spontaneous,** nervous, **capable,*** leader,* **calm,*** persevering, **controlled,*** sensitive, hate regulations,* **independent,*** lack self-confidence, irritable,* patient, **tolerant**

The present status of the client is preparation for a third career, or phase of life. Her teaching in secondary schools plus teaching occasional extension courses for colleges and universities provides intact skills if she wishes to use them. Her writing is judged to be on at least a high avocational level. Family health is good, and her husband has steadily improved his professional and financial situation. The oldest son is close to the Ph.D. degree in the biological sciences, the middle boy graduates from college this year. The youngest son is meeting his military obligations after two years of successful college work and will return to college the coming year.

The Psychologist's Corner

Mrs. A-3 represents a larger number of individuals than is generally supposed. She knows herself quite well. The level of reality testing is high. She is in touch with her environment, cultures, and subcultures beyond the half-generation "turtle shell." Her insight into the third dynamic relating self and environment, and their interactions, is exceptional. Why bother with a psychologist at all? One answer is that the action is a reflection of life-style. The need for adaptation and adjustment to a new period of life is clear to her. She is self-confident, capable, and independent. If she wishes to build a house, she sees an architect. If her car doesn't run well, she consults a mechanic. If she wishes more information about herself and her environment, she consults the specialist she perceives as most appropriate.

Miss A-4

Age 55; unmarried; 16 years of formal education

Evaluation: methodical planning for early retirement, no psychotherapeutic indicators, minimum IQ equivalent 125

Miss A-4 was a career woman. Efficient, hard working, intelligent, and apparently not too dismayed at not becoming a housewife, she accepted a position with a state agency almost immediately upon graduation from college at age twenty-one. Her major was the general humanities. She climbed quite rapidly from high-level quasi-clerical chores to administrative responsibilities in dealing with people. Miss A-4 has been accepted equally well working with either men or women, passing the crucial test for a female administrator by employing, and keeping, male employees of considerable ability.

Miss A-4 went through her childhood and early teens on a family cattle ranch. While her older sister married and moved some distance from the family home, her younger brother has maintained the ranch. Miss A-4 has developed no strong avocational outlets other than a deep amateur interest in the ranch. She has spent many vacation periods there and considered it her "real" home. Although Miss A-4 has not been a joiner, she has been a member of two professional organizations, holding local offices.

Miss A-4 claimed to have no particular problems other than a desire to plan for retirement in the relatively near future. At fifty-five she already had thirty-four years of service with the state agency. The retirement arrangements were reasonably adequate financially. In addition, she had purchased annuities and made investments which appeared to provide ample retirement security. The comparison of client-psychologist dimensions of self-actualization is below.

Self-actualizing dimensions	*Self-rating, percentile*	*Psychologist rating, percentile*
Efficiency variables	90	90
Self-expression	90	90
Leadership	85	75
Performance vs. potential	85	95
Social-political	90	95
Social contribution	70	90
Self-sufficiency	75	90
Creativity	70	75
Maturity	90	95
Social-vocational multipotentiality	85	90

Miss A-4 reflected the cues of life-style in other ways. Her indication of terms which she believed applied to her reinforces data from other sources.

excitable, depressed, **sociable,*** **sense of humor,*** **hard working,*** shy, love excitement, **conscientious,*** **ambitious,*** dreamer,* **happy,*** worried, **confident,*** **reserved,** spontaneous, nervous, **capable,*** **leader, calm,*** **persevering,*** **controlled,*** **sensitive,** hate regulations, **independent,*** lack self-confidence, irritable, **patient,*** **tolerant***

The present status of Miss A-4 is the final year of work at age fifty-eight. She plans to keep an apartment in the city but live part of the first retirement year with her brother and his family on the ranch. Psychoevaluation uncovered no startling new directions, but rather confirmed what she already perceived about herself, her environment, and her place in it for the next several years. She wants the tryout of the ranch life to see whether or not there are aspects which may revive her interests of an earlier age.

The Psychologist's Corner

Miss A-4 reflects her life-style throughout the professional relationship with the psychologist. She is methodical. Her planning for retirement, like her vocational career planning, is long-circuited. She sees quite clearly the probable difficulties ahead, considers the alternatives, studies the major dimensions involved, and is prepared in advance for what happens. Perhaps the most striking aspect is her calm reality testing, not only of the present but also of what may well come to be. But while the term methodical has somewhat pedestrian qualities, Miss A-4 is not a mousy, colorless person, quite the contrary.

A SUMMARY FOR THE LADIES

Four brief case reviews have been presented involving normal, mature, self-actualizing women. No attempt was made to include the mass of data upon which the reviews were based. In each case the client-psychologist estimates of the dimensions of self-actualization used in this book were presented. In some instances these estimates were reached after interview discussion of the dimensions. In other instances personal documents supplied the information. Because the psychologist was not in formal private practice and no fees were involved, the relationship may have differed in some important aspects from cases where a formal, fee paying process supplies part of the relationship structure.

Although there is no special mention of psychometrics beyond interest inventories, appropriate tests of academic ability, values, and goals were used with one or more of the clients in varied patterns. The inclusion of such measurement results was not considered of particular importance for the purpose of these reviews. Once again, it is emphasized that each of these women would have reached socially and personally acceptable solutions to her problems of adaptation and distribution without the help of a psychologist, psychiatrist, or other professional behavioral scientist. This is not to say that there are not benefits for many from professional services. Savings in time, release from choice-anxieties, earlier movement toward solutions for difficult personal problems, and the satisfactions to be derived from professional support perceived as reality testing—all contribute to the needs and wants of those seeking psychoevaluation.

THE MILITARY

Men and women in military uniform are not particularly conspicuous to the public in times of peace. Relatively few people have the opportunity to observe at close range the quality of those who follow a professional military career. Many of us are aware of the difficult entrance requirements and the stiff curricula of West Point, Annapolis, the Air Force Academy, and the Coast Guard Academy. We sometimes fail to note the graduates of excellent colleges and universities who also select a military career. And even less noted are the enlisted personnel who move toward the top—the "mustangs." It seems reasonable to believe that position for position, men and women in the military measure up in all regards to those who make their careers in business and industry, education, and governmental services. The military group is of special interest because it is the rule, not the exception, that those who resign or retire plan for, prepare, and enter second and even third careers.

It is a temptation to use cases which are startling to illustrate the points stressed in this section. For example, at a recent social event there were present a man of sixty-one and his wife of fifty-seven. The husband resigned from a captain's commission in the navy during his late forties. He entered business as an accounting specialist in a large Eastern city. Highly successful financially, but having lost interest, he "retired" again at age fifty-nine. The wife was a successful homemaker and mother. When her husband retired the first time, she also entered business in personnel work. Now the two of them are simultaneously working toward Ph.D. degrees in a major university. However, we will present our thumbnail case histories about able individuals who are more typical.

The three representative cases in this section provided common psychometric information only in regard to the Army General Classification Test. The lowest raw score was 146 and the highest 157. For this test the mean is a raw score of 100, and the standard deviation is 20. Because of rank, only one was required by his branch of service to accomplish the instrument. The others requested personal administration out of curiosity. Two also completed the Kuder Preference Record which was being used experimentally. None wrote life histories or structured autobiographies. Each was known to the writer for a period of more than ten years. Although there were many personal conferences in various settings, the formal interview situation was never involved. Psychoevaluation was involved, but in a manner which was most unorthodox.

B-1

Age 45; married; 1 child; 14 years of formal education

Evaluation: choice-anxiety; intact career and avocational outlets; coinciding interests, achievements, aptitudes, and abilities; minimum IQ equivalent 130

The client was a mustang who began his military career as a private. He married late, and the son was ten years of age at the time the relationship with a psychologist began. The wife was a professional woman. B-1 completed two years of college, was very unhappy with the formal collegiate setting, and dropped his formal education to enlist in the military service. His academic record was brilliant where he was interested and felt that his teachers "had something to say." In courses where the criteria of interest and teaching eminence were not met, the record was indifferent.

Although there were several opportunities, or perhaps urgings by superior officers, to become a commissioned officer during a long career as a noncommissioned officer, all were rejected. During World War II a commission was accepted because his competence in a specialty was too critical to be used except with the commission. The military record was outstanding, including a more than average number of citations and medals. Retirement was voluntary before the age limits for active service were met. His wife continued her professional work for a period of five years after B-1 retired.

Self-actualizing dimensions	*Self-rating, percentile*	*Psychologist rating, percentile*
Efficiency variables	90	98
Self-expression	95	95
Leadership (military)	95	95
Performance vs. potential (military)	95	95
(civilian)	70	60
Social-political	75	95
Social contribution (civilian)	65	50
Self-sufficiency	95	100
Creativity	95	98
Maturity	95	70
Social-vocational multipotentiality	95	95

In many ways B-1 was the most complex person with whom the writer has dealt professionally. The social-vocational multipotentiality was so great that it might be classified as a detriment. B-1 was an example of an ideal self-educated person. The range and depth of reading over a long period of time included engineering and mechanics, philosophy, anthropology, history, psychology, and literature. Present too, was a self-taught trilinguality with proficiency in reading, speaking, and writing. The elements of leadership were outstanding when they were put to use, but there was little interest in a leadership role.

In terms of achievement the picture was consistent. Transfer of the military skills to civilian life would have required little, if any, formal retraining or education. B-1 was an engineer of no mean status without formal preparation. He wrote exceedingly well in both technical and nontechnical matters. The untrained potentials in the graphic arts were judged by informed people in the field as outstanding. His record in instructional situations indicated great ability as a teacher. Several years after an original close personal relationship, B-1 is working in a creative capacity for his own personal satisfaction. His work, according to critics, is excellent and would easily provide a livelihood if B-1 wished to make a career in the field. Finances are no particular problem so there is no need to earn additional money to meet the family needs and wants as they are perceived.

The Psychologist's Corner

It was too easy to reach logical, but false, conclusions about B-1. At various times the appraisal suggested terms such as "rigid," "cynical," "arrogant," "asocial," and "sadistic." But he was none of these. Rigidity disappeared when interest was involved. Cynicism was a mask. Arrogance was impatience with those whose cerebrations were markedly below his own, and this extended to a large proportion of his fellow citizens. There was a sad contempt for humanity in general but a facility for warm relationships with people whom he liked and respected. He was asocial if individuals were not interesting to him and could not communicate with him at his very high least common denominator. B-1 was brutally frank. If he detected superficiality or pomposity, his quiet verbal mayhem was awesome. Early in the personal relationship some thought was given to psychotherapy. This was quickly discarded both because longer acquaintanceship did not support the diagnosis and to protect any psychotherapist who might be tempted.

B-1 was self-actualizing in his military career by all three criteria—self-judgment, judgment of peers, and judgment of specialist. Whether or not he retained this status as a civilian is a matter of opinion. He perceives himself so, and for him this is truth and reality. There is no access to civilian peers. Psychologist judgment is that he is contributing socially far below his potential, but this is his personal affair.

The services rendered to B-1 included bibliocommunication, privileged communication, and information. Bibliocommunication centered on providing or recommending reading material on subjects of interest to B-1, or which were thought of as supplementary to his interests. B-1 seldom let down the guard about his personal feelings. Because he understood privileged communication, the psychologist was used as a sounding board when there was a need to talk. B-1 made certain the psychologist was nondirective! Over a number of years the psychologist was asked to provide information in a number of directions. These requests for information appeared to come only when B-1 had exhausted his own considerable resources for obtaining it. Often the requests took the form of asking for information as to how to obtain information.

B-2

Age 48; married; 5 children; 13 years of formal education

Evaluation: lack of information; lack of skill; coinciding interests, achievements, aptitudes, and abilities; minimum IQ equivalent 135

Mr. B-2, like B-1, was a mustang. An outstanding athlete, he was injured during his freshman year of college and enlisted as a private in the military. He married quite young. The five children are four boys and a girl. All of the children have demonstrated unusual academic potential. The wife has had no career or job preparation or experience. She was unusually successful as a wife and mother using Terman's criteria. B-2 emerged from World War II with a satisfying number of ribbons and medals coupled with the essential battle stars.

B-2 moved rapidly up the NCO ladder, was selected for officer training, and was promoted ahead of schedule in the commissioned ranks. At the end of the war he decided that civilian life would be a welcome change and, after twenty-seven years of military life, resigned his commission. B-2 knew what he wanted to do. He completed the B.A. and the M.S. and entered on a doctoral program in near record-breaking time. He is engaged in teaching and research in higher education while completing the doctorate. Three of the children, including the daughter, have graduated from college. The two younger boys are in college. The graduates all earned academic honors, and the two "in process" are following the same trails.

Self-actualizing dimensions	*Self-rating, percentile*	*Psychologist rating, percentile*
Efficiency variables	85	95
Self-expression	90	95
Leadership (military)	75	90
(civilian)	50	75
Performance vs. potential (both military and civilian)	90	95
Social-political	85	90
Social contribution (civilian)	75	85
Self-sufficiency	90	95
Creativity (organization-management)	80	90
Maturity	95	90
Social-vocational multipotentiality	75	90

B-2 is particularly self-actualizing in his ability to test reality in both military and civilian situations and environments and create novel, practical solutions. Although his interests center very strongly about activities in formal higher education, the life pattern leads one to believe he would be equally successful in business and industrial management which demands rapid decision making at a policy level. He has been, and is, truly creative in this regard. B-2 writes exceedingly well when dealing with materials which explain and describe. His writing leads one to believe that a career could be carved here. Certainly writing offers a fine avocational outlet.

The Psychologist's Corner

B-2 exemplifies the self-sufficiency so characteristic of military officers who come through the system. Although lack of information is a legitimate descriptive term regarding B-2, the information desired was of a sort which indicated an excellent knowledge and appraisal of personal dynamics. "I know what I want, and where I am going! What is the shortest legitimate road to take?" In the same manner, lack of skill has its own flavor. The skills of teaching were already present. What was really needed was the pieces of paper, diplomas and certificates, which certified that they were present. The chief services rendered by the psychologist were those related to saving time with just a bit of confirmation of choice.

B-3

Age 46; married; 3 children; 16 years of formal education

Evaluation: choice-anxiety, lack of information, shift of military administrative skills to civilian use, minimum IQ equivalent 130

B-3 entered the military through a university Reserve Officers Training program. His only career has been military. He married his college sweetheart. There are three girls—fourteen, seventeen, and nineteen years of age. Mrs. B-3 completed three years of college in a general humanities program and then married. She has had no premarriage career and has not worked up to this time. B-3 had become increasingly stifled by the monotony of the peacetime military. His combat record during World War II was excellent.

Since the end of the war his competence as an administrator has made him "chair bound." His head is against the ceiling of promotion. Although one more promotion is thought to be on the way eventually, B-3 "wants out." He can retire with twenty-five years of service. Like so many other men from the military, he is considering teaching in secondary schools as a first civilian staging area.

Oral and written communications yield the following comparisons on the dimensions of self-actualization we are using.

Self-actualizing dimensions	*Self-rating, percentile*	*Psychologist rating, percentile*
Efficiency variables	90	90
Self-expression	60	65
Leadership (*military*)	95	80
Performance vs. potential (*military*)	70	85
Social-political	90	90
Social contributions	60	55
Self-sufficiency	95	95
Creativity	70	65
Maturity	90	90
Social-vocational multipotentiality	80	90

B-3 has his high points for self-actualization on the efficiency variables, social-political balance, self-sufficiency, and maturity. Other data support the conclusion that his present career skills can be converted, almost intact, into business, industrial, or governmental administrative activities. B-3 has begun graduate work in professional education following his retirement. While he has been successful in the academic setting, he is not obligated to use the experience only in the direction of teaching in a secondary school.

The Psychologist's Corner

B-3, like B-1 and B-2, is an example of a person who will find his way without professional help. Lack of information has not been a serious handicap as he knew where to obtain information which was perceived as relevant for adaptation to civilian life. Lack of assurance was in large part a function of lack of information. The lack of skills is a matter of specificity where the problems can be met in a rather short period of time. Psychologist help may have shortened time needed to strike balance as a civilian by from six months to a year. It would be difficult to prove that the quality of choice has been improved. Prediction—an administrator, probably in business and industry, within a year or two.

THOSE WHO ARE NEITHER LADIES NOR RETIRED FROM THE MILITARY

This all-male group is presented as representative of various efforts at coping behavior in several situational matrices. The examples are selected from those who have wanted communication with a professional worker for a number of reasons. Privileged communication has been a factor. Academic and professional status symbols have played a part. Word of mouth "advertising" by "satisfied customers" was in evidence. Lack of assurance brought others seeking an opportunity for reality testing under nonthreatening circumstances. A number of mature men and women come in or write or telephone simply because they believe that one has information which is needed. Often these information seekers follow up by disclosing other needs which they believe that a psychologist can and will meet. As one would expect, individuals with more or less serious adjustment difficulties also appeared. Within the writer's diagnostic competence, these were referred to adjustment psychologists.

The form followed on previous pages will not be followed in this section. A statement of reasons for communication will be given together with some population data. A general outline of the life history will be included but, by and large, the whole presentation will be of the nature of "the psychologist's corner." As in all of these thumbnail presentations, information is altered in a manner to prevent identification of the individuals.

C-1

Age 42; married; 2 children; 13 years of formal education

Evaluation: lack of information, minimum IQ equivalent 120
Self-actualizing high points: efficiency variables, leadership, performance vs. potential, social contribution, self-sufficiency, creativity, social-vocational multipotentiality
Attainment of early goals: power over others, financial rewards, security, personal satisfaction (for the sowing period)
Values: a shift from an egocentric, materialistic orientation to a higher valuing of social service

C-1 had left college at the end of his first year for a number of reasons including a "Joe College" attitude, mediocre grades, and the best interests of the college as judged by the administration. He entered business at the bottom, moved through production, sales, and management, organized his own enterprise, and was highly successful. He became bored with the routines of running a business. Having achieved more than modest wealth, he looked around and decided that there were things to be done in "contributing to a better society."

Although C-1 had chosen a general direction, he had begun a systematic investigation of route. Communication with the writer centered about checking his own self-understanding and images, validating his remarkably good understandings of the second dynamic, and spending time and effort on the interaction dynamics for a new field and an individual with changed goals—services to others—and shifting value system loadings. There appeared to be no serious difficulties in adjustment. There were three interviews and two letters from C-1, one letter being a brief life history and its evaluation. Bibliocommunication entered the process through recommended reading. C-1 apparently found the information he sought and carried through with his plans. As one would expect from the life-style, his contributions were financial and managerial using the skills developed and exercised successfully in his business career. The psychological service rendered appears to be that of helping with certain kinds of reality testing, a sounding board for thinking out loud, and the saving of client time in moving in a direction in which he would have gone without professional consultation.

C-2

Age 35; married but separated; no children; 16 years of formal education, foreign citizen (Asiatic)

Evaluation: lack of information, lack of assurance, intercultural conflict

Self-actualization high points: efficiency variables, self-sufficiency, social-vocational multipotentiality, maturity

Early and present goals: personal satisfaction, service to others, security

Values: imbedded in an Eastern religious philosophy. Psychologist lacked backgrounds and competence to make valid assumptions

C-2 was a man who had moved surely and smoothly to the respect of his peers and to status of a reasonably high order in his culture. He had obtained permission to enter the United States as a quota immigrant. C-2 came to the writer "to understand his new homeland better." He was a college graduate. Although he was trilingual, his secondary and higher education was in English which he spoke, read, and wrote fluently. Although his major stated difficulties lay primarily in the adaptation area, there were unmistakable signs of adjustment problems. At no time during the relationship was there any attempt at formal psychotherapy because the client appeared in good control of the masks. Whatever psychotherapeutic aid was given was through dealing with the adaptation loadings.

Unlike in the other cases in this chapter, psychometric devices were used in a setting of assessment. Two interest inventories, two American intelligence tests, one personality inventory, and the Allport-Vernon-Lindzey Scale of Values were administered. Clinical inference was, of course, strained beyond the breaking point as the norms for American subjects have no known relationship to the culture of C-2. In terms of this single person the responses to items and the scale patterns were quite consistent with what would be expected of such a person in our Western culture. In addition to the tests, scales, and inventories, cited above, C-2 wrote a life history (8,000 words) and a structured autobiography. Interviews consumed some twelve hours. The client based the final interview on a psychologist-written report to C-2 (3,000+ words). Responses to specific test and inventory items were also used at times for discussion purposes. Some bibliocommunication was employed as reasonably good libraries were available in the English language.

The intelligence test results, both power and speed scores having been obtained, indicated an average level for four-year college graduates in the United States. There was no way to estimate the effect of taking these instruments in a second language or the effect of obviously out-of-culture items included in the instruments. The interest inventories gave patterns which were consonant with his career. The life pattern teased out of the life history and the autobiographical materials was consistent with scores on both the interest inventories and the scale of values.

C-2 did come to the United States. The last follow-up indicated that he had landed on his feet and was establishing himself in a Western culture both vocationally and socially. At the time of last report there had been no serious adjustment problems. As indicated, the adaptation and distribution areas were being adequately handled. Because there was involvement in all four of the normality indicators, the psychologist probably contributed to an unknown extent to information, skills, and alleviated choice-anxiety in certain directions. Although C-2 would have come to the United States under any circumstances, it appears that he came with more assurance and less anxiety than would have been the case had there been no relationship to a psychologist. He probably saved time in his adaptations in the United States, and there may have been a substantial reduction in anxiety regarding finding a place.

C-3

Age 48; married; 3 children, son, two daughters; 17 years of formal education

Evaluation: self-conflict, professional trap, minimum IQ equivalent 130
Self-actualization high points: efficiency variables, self-sufficiency, social-vocational multipotentiality, creativity
Early goals: personal satisfaction, security
Present adaptation goals: financial rewards, power over others
Values: family, professional integrity

C-3 is almost a perfect example of Pepinsky's (1948, 101) *Self-Conflict* category and the Darley Hagenah (1955) *professional trap.* Pepinsky (1948) describes the category characteristics in part as:

> Clients with *Self-Conflict* are alike in that they have conflicting motivations to action. White (1941), like Stern, refers to these motivations as "goal-directed" strivings; conflict results when a client has "strivings" which impels him to incompatible modes of action.
>
> Jung's concept of ambivalence helps to explain the nature of such conflict. Thus an individual may be motivated toward a course of action which is in line with his own desires, and at the same time, toward an alternative course of action in line with an opposed set of desires, either his own or imposed upon him by his culture in which he desires status and security.

C-3 began and developed a career as an engineer with a real flair for experimentation and research. His creativity made him an important figure in the large corporation by which he was employed upon the completion of his bachelor's degree in engineering with one year of graduate work. When World War II began, there was need for a man who had a very high level of professional and technical competence in mechanical and electrical engineering to represent the company in the negotiation of government contracts. C-3, against his will, stepped into the position on what he thought was a temporary assignment. He was too successful. He learned the roles of the super salesman and played them with distinction.

During the period between the war's end and 1952 he demonstrated his ability to obtain nongovernmental contracts in stiff competition. His gross income rose to impressive heights. However, he undertook the support of relatives from both sides of the family. The son and one daughter entered relatively expensive colleges. The boy was a junior and the daughter a sophomore in college, each well established in the institution attended. The drain on even his seemingly ample income was exceedingly heavy.

His recourse to a psychologist was prompted by a consuming, and increasing, hatred for the roles which made his income possible. The Strong Vocational Interest Blank yielded an almost perfect stereotype of the engineer's interest pattern. How much faking, conscious or unconscious, might have entered into the completion of this inventory is not known. The results fitted extremely well into the life history and life-style. His attempts to escape the sales-promotional trap included negotiations to return to his laboratory. The employing industry was reluctantly willing to permit this second shift of career pattern. The shift, however, would almost halve his income. C-3 believed that if he could hang on until the daughter now in college received her degree, he could rearrange his scale of living and make-do on the reduced income. This would mean a less expensive education for the youngest daughter who would enter college in the next year.

At best C-3 could race time against a possible serious adjustment problem. To the psychologist there seemed a real danger of a crippling personality disintegration. C-3 refused to consider referral to a psychotherapist. "He could carry the load by himself." He was proud of his adaptation and worried seriously about his adjustment. C-3 did last through to the graduation of the first daughter. Touch was lost at about this period, and no follow-up was available at the time this was written.

IN SUMMARY

In this chapter ten brief reports about normal, mature, self-actualizing people have been presented. Three categories were used—the ladies, retired military men, and those who did not fall into either of the other groups. Full data about the individuals were withheld both for purposes of concealing identity and because the purpose of the chapter was not to present cases "for practice." In one instance, C-3, the psychotherapy indicators were judged to be heavily involved. But even in this instance a satisfactory adaptation to the key situation might permit the person to maintain adjustment equilibrium and improve the present imbalances. Pepinsky's (1948) normality indicators, lack of information, lack of assurance, lack of skill, and choice-anxiety were used to classify the adaptation problem areas. With C-3 the *self-conflict* psychotherapy category was used.

Chapter 6

PROCESS

In chapter 1 process in psychoevaluation was briefly outlined. The purpose of this chapter is to present in some detail the discussions with which to clothe the earlier skeleton. As was also stated in Chapter 1, the process of psychoevaluation is perceived by the writer as being at two levels of psychological complexity and purpose. The psychologist practicing psychoevaluation is assumed to be competent in human *assessment* as described and defined in Chapters 1 and 9. Assessment includes prediction against criteria for (usually) specific ends such as school admission or promotion or employment. Although this prediction is in terms of future behavior dynamics, its basis is present relative statics. Psychological counseling, which frequently accompanies assessment, seldom provides the opportunity for involved communication or communication techniques because of the age group and content with which most of this counseling is done. Clients in the decades of *becoming* differ qualitatively in a number of ways from those in the decades of *being* and *having been.*

The second, and more complex level, evaluation, uses the methods and data of assessment in various ways. But the greater complexity arises from such considerations as the lack of appropriate psychometric devices, normative materials, changed and changing values and life goals, and the differences in client-psychologist relationships growing out of age and maturity. Greater emphasis is placed on societal dynamics and on using methods of communication of wider range and greater depth than is usually true with younger, less mature clients. *Psychoevaluation,* which differs from evaluation in purpose but has a close relationship in methodology, was defined in Chapter 1. In this chapter we are concerned with the major dimensions of psychoevaluation as a process. Our discussion is presented under the rubrics of *relationship, process content,* and *communication.*

RELATIONSHIP

Relationship between a client and a psychologist involves among other dimensions the roles, masks, status symbols, personality, emotions, and the perceptions of each. No matter how many other variables of some possible weight we might specify, a fairly broad area of ambiguity would still remain for the client. Much of the meaning of relationship lies in the answer to the simple question the client addresses to himself, "Why am I here?"

The literature contains much material in the field of psychotherapy which attempts to define and describe relationship. A recommended example is W. U. Snyder's *The Psychotherapy Relationship* (1961). Chapters 1 and 14 are of particular pertinence. Snyder indicates relationship differences among and between various approaches to psychotherapy. He indicates also some lines of cleavage between psychotherapy and its "normal" relatives, counseling and psychoevaluation.

When relationship has been discussed in the literature of dealing with the normal, the tendency has been to avoid psychotherapeutic terms. For example, Cottle and Downie (1960, 62) describe relationship briefly when they say:

> After the client has been made reasonably comfortable physically and psychologically, the counselor begins the process of creating a climate of confidence and trust. Whether or not the term "rapport" is used to describe this, or whether this goal is stated as providing a "warm, permissive atmosphere" the relationship must be based on *mutual* respect and willing cooperation.

Pepinsky and Pepinsky (1954, 64) use a broader interpretation of relationship, based, in part, on psychotherapeutic concepts. They state:

> *Client-counselor "talk" and "relationship" are basic.* In three articles Shoben has stressed the importance of these two variables in all counseling approaches. Talk is simply the conversational content of interviews. Relationship is an atmosphere of mutual acceptance in which the counselor is able to indicate his understanding and nonjudgmental attitudes toward the client. How the relationship is to be manipulated is still an issue.

Hahn and MacLean (1955, 83) use rapport as a synonym for relationship:

> Rapport, for our purposes, means sustained interest and mutual understanding and respect between two human beings who are analyzing together, and seeking solutions for, a problem important to the one because it is *his* problem and to the other because it is his job to help. Expenditure of whatever time is necessary to establish this relationship in a preliminary interview or interviews is justified. On the part of the counselee it involves developing a feeling of ease, born of growing confidence in the counselor's competence, interest, knowledge, and skill and a feeling of freedom to reveal both facts and emotions. On the part of the counselor it entails treating the (counselee) as a responsible adult, being considerate of all attitudes and feelings, resistant to shock whatever may be said. He must be patient in the face of repetition, indecision, or inconsistency and sensitive to the timing of his questions and

comments. He must use sharp retorts and critical comments or warm and tender sympathetic ones only as tools, not as expressions of his own emotions, temper, judgments, or morals.

However, neither the descriptions of relationship in psychotherapy nor counseling exactly fit our client as described in Chapters 4 and 5. In psychotherapy there is the clear intent of doing something to, or for, the patient. His anxieties are to be reduced or better controlled, his overt social behavior is to be changed, his attitudinal sets altered, and his resistance to change overcome, no matter how gently and subtly. Some ambiguity exists for many patients between the *patient-physician* and the *patient-psychologist* roles.

In counseling psychology, relationship is affected to an unknown extent by assessment *for* something. Age differences tend to influence the situation, status of the psychologist as *being* in the face of the client's *becoming* may have impact, the need to fill gaps in essential knowledge introduces elements of possible importance, and the narrow line between counseling and advising at some points must be ignored.

Relationship, as it applies to the interview in business and industrial situations, does not appear to have great application in counseling, psychotherapy, or psychoevaluation. Both the interviewer and the interviewee "want something," and the dimensions of the relationship often include a jockeying for position to gain one's ends.

Roe (1956), in the report of her first year of a four-year study, does introduce elements of significance in this context. She dealt with mature, normal individuals, albeit in a research setting. Her reports of the case histories and other data indicate that, by and large, self-actualization characterized her population. Aside from the fact that she approached her subjects (clients), instead of their seeking her, many of the conditions of relationship in psychoevaluation were present.

In considering relationship in psychoevaluation, it is most difficult to avoid beginning a description with the trite, but essential, words—*warm, accepting,* and *open.* Personal experience suggests also the word "reserved" for the psychologist's role. Because a major element concerns cognition, and vigilance is a not uncommon characteristic of our clients, reserve is important, particularly in the first interviews. The importance of client control of outcomes, coupled with the psychologist control of general process structure, introduces a sometimes shuttlecock-like passing of the leadership role in the interviews. When provision of personal data is the chief focus, the client is unquestionably the leader and knower. Interpretation of data is a joint venture. Placement of interpretations within a psychological structure is, at least part of the time, a chiefly psychologist function. Many clients are as old as, or older than, the psychologist. This in itself dictates some dimensions of relationship.

As has been said earlier, transference and countertransference, will not usually be of importance. Feeling tone and affect will be present but as facilitators of communication, not necessarily as integral and important contributors to the success or failure of the process. One danger to relationship is the role of the psychologist in aiding client self-actualization when lack of information, skills, or assurance is important. Pedantic roles are seldom well received. Another danger is the shift of the psychologist's role to that of psychotherapist when unforeseen interview situations permit, or cause, client masks to slip. There are times when this role shift is wise and necessary, but one should be cautious in the timing of role change and in its duration.

In closing these comments on relationship in psychoevaluation, three more words are added with differential client-psychologist loadings—*respect, confidence,* and *liking*. The reader may feel lack of closure because anxiety has not been introduced in the discussion. This is the case on the grounds that, while anxiety must be present or the client would not have become a client, it is long-circuited anxiety, tending to be more vague than is ordinarily encountered in clients and patients. While its triggers often are specific foreseen possibilities, it is not close to fear. If we consider anxiety as a desirable and essential condition for psychological survival, and it is within an optimal range, its client-psychologist manipulation is seldom of primary importance.

PROCESS CONTENT

Process content in psychoevaluation will be, in large part, client-originated. The description of past behavior will contribute the raw data for evaluating life-style. Many of the dimensions of the relative statics will come from analysis of client-prepared material. Personality structure and assessment, while a contribution of the psychologist, also demand quite heavy client contributions. In terms of crisis situations, the psychologist should bring to the process an understanding and knowledge of the cultural and subcultural history of recent times. Crisis impact must come from the client's information. The clarification of the dynamics of personal and environmental interaction will tend to lie in the psychologist's domain because of his role as structurer. Final planning, which frequently involves verbalizing by the client relative to his choices of alternatives, is almost completely the client's.

In dealing with process content the psychologist approaches the concepts of statistical reliability and validity of data in a frame of reference different, in some ways, from that of those who are chiefly concerned with the distributive and adjustive aspects of practice. Where employment or job promotion assessment is involved, test scores, items in the personal work and educational history, and information regarding social participation should meet the usual tests of verifiability and relationship to predetermined criteria. In situations where diagnosis for psychotherapy is necessary, the diagnosing psychologist or psychiatrist must have some methods of insuring the integrity of the data from which he can make prognoses and plan therapeutic measures aimed at cure or change. In psychoevaluation, however, because there is no psychologizing *to* or *for* a specific objective, the need to consider reliability and validity of data for the *with* is not identical with the examples cited above. The client is in charge; much of what happens is at the cognitive level. Prediction, in the sense it is used by the psychologist at the assessment level, is of a quite different kind. If, for any reason, the client wishes to hold his masks so tightly to his overt behavior that he gives himself false information to avoid self-revelation, then, perhaps, there should be a *diagnosis* to indicate the possible need for psychotherapy. Strict adherence to standard concepts of reliability and validity is not necessary in order that the psychologist provide structure within which the client may understand himself and his environment better. For self-distribution and adaptation to changed, and changing, internal and external conditions related to psychological and physiological maturing and aging, we deal with the levels of cognitive insight and roles to a large extent.

RELATIVE STATICS

The term *relative statics* is used to designate relevant past conditions represented by items of information such as bits from the life history, or test scores. In systematic case studies of individuals, it is necessary to take a series of cross-section samplings, at various times, in order to judge future movement and changes (dynamics). We refer to a related and integrated series of cross-sectional assessments as a "longitudinal" case study. The analogy here is to a motion picture film. Shown at proper speed the picture on the screen is dynamic; it moves and interactions are easily observed. If, however, we take single frames of the film and look at them through a viewer, we have stills, or statics. In a single frame much of the interaction of players, plots, and actions disappear. One of the seemingly essential methodologies of studying dynamics, for example the wing movements of a humming bird, is by a series of statics with proper temporal relationships.

If our concern is with intrapersonal cross sections (adjustment), inference plays a larger role than is true of interpersonal, environmental cross sections where direct observation aids us to some extent in our inferences. The interpretation of data and patternings of data always is an outcome of inference, buttressed, as well as possible, by reference to nomothetic approaches.

The Relative Statics of Life-style

Both Super (1957) and Maslow (1954) attend to life-styles, patterns, or flavors, with emphasis on the concepts as keys to the understanding of an individual by others. This approach also permeates Gordon Allport's writings (1937, 1950, 1955, 1960). The patterns of relatively consistent and temporally persistent behavior do emerge if methods are used which afford a longitudinal view. In longitudinal studies of individuals, the psychologist finds axes and focal points which, with proper interpretation, clarify meaning, give insights, and provide content and concepts communicable to the client.

The poles about which patterns appear to cluster differ somewhat among and between men and women. As has been indicated earlier, for the male, psychological health and survival focus strongly in our culture on the occupational area. Status symbols, important feedback, and the exploratory forces intersect for many in this strongly affective behavior center. Much of this is a recapitulation of what is contained in Chapter 2. The concern here is use of the materials as content for client-psychologist structuring.

Not only are the methods of collecting the data important, as will be seen later, but the axes along which it is collected are also of moment for client self-insight and self-actualization. A developmental axis is obvious. What have been the way stations from the first employment of a significant nature to what the client perceives as the peak? A satisfaction axis is indicated—at what points, in what life periods, was satisfaction from the job functions perceived as greatest? Where were the status symbols most rewarding? What kinds of symbols? How is the present occupational status perceived relative to the past and the near future?

For many women, the career as a homemaker holds the same meaning as the occupational symbols do for the male. Support for this is found in considerations of the Strong Vocational Interest Blank, for example, in the writing of Hoppock (1935), Darley and Hagenah (1955), Strong (1943), Super (1949), Cottle and Downie (1960) and Roe (1956), Terman and Oden (1959). Here, as has been stated earlier, in a manner quite different from the withdrawal of men from occupations, the mother role with its deep emotional roots usually begins a quite rapid change when the youngest child obtains his or her driving license.

From the life-style data one can also infer and trace changed and changing life goals and values. These dimensions are, of course, enmeshed with the numerous other nets and circuits of the central nervous system and its affective aspects. Stagner (1961, 333) calls attention to the importance of goals in adult behavior:

> Adult behavior, by contrast, shows persistent goal orientation lasting over years. The quest for a profession, political ambition, and many other kinds of life patterns illustrate this enduring characteristic. It seems much more realistic, therefore, to describe human behavior, particularly at the level of enduring organizations which make up personality, as a goal-seeking process rather than as a response to biogenic drives.

Other personality statics of importance to client and psychologist in the process of psychoevaluation are those of traits and trait patterns. (Temperaments are included as traits.) Formal education level and type have a bearing on the life history as do evidences of sensory deprivation in the crucial childhood years. The individual's relative status in his "turtle shell" of a half generation in which he competes economically and politically, and participates socially, must be considered as pertinent data.

Always, in reviewing and interpreting the personality statics, their possible uses in present and future dynamics must be considered. This has strong application in planning nonvocational outlets for time and energy whether retirement is imminent or, at present, a distant prospect to be considered at some leisure. In this light, attention to possible avocations and hobbies may merit consideration. Super (1940) and Havighurst and Albrecht (1953) have written valuable materials on these topics. We quote Super (1957, 159) to emphasize our concern with planning ahead:

> Since preretirement occupations and adjustments vary so, and since the process of decline manifests itself so differently and at such different ages, retirement means different things to different people. It may mean unwelcome inactivity, or freedom to do things one has not had the time to do, or escape from pressures that are too great. Retirement requires

changing the habits and daily routines of a lifetime, changing a self-concept which has been relatively stable over a long period of years, and changing a role which has been played for more than a generation. Old roles such as those of a worker and parent are reduced, and others such as those of a homemaker and church member are intensified.

If we perceive the above quotation in the light of Cattell's "Newton's law of psychology," our resistance to change really suffers some cataclysmic shocks, and the battle for psychological adaptation and survival produces casualties.

To this point we have considered clients and their relative statics of personality as a quite homogeneous group with subgroups labeled *male* and *female*. However, it is obvious that skin color, religion, and racial ancestry also introduce client subgroups who must face, throughout the life-span, both personal and environmental conditions which yield perceptions, values, and goals quite different from a dominant white, Caucasian, protestant majority. Few psychologists have the experience to deal expertly with these client subgroups: Negroes, orthodox Jews, Mormons, Catholics, those of Japanese-American heritage or of Spanish-American origin, and, the writer is tempted to include, college and university faculty members.

One must also be aware of important differences between Beacon Hill, Boston, and Beacon Street, Memphis, as points of origin. Georgia and Montana; New York City and Pea Ridge, Arkansas; Oak Ridge and Scranton—these variables all have some importance in working with individuals whose major period of becoming and being were spent in known geographical and subcultural areas with distinctive flavors. To the extent one accepts determinism, it is operating along these dimensions as well as others.

Environmental Statics

It will be impossible to do more here than to sketch broad dimensions of concern. Another book is needed, and planned, to focus on culture and subculture, adaptation and adjustment. Several times in the materials encountered earlier, attention has been called to the tendency of individuals in the Western culture to move in a half generation of time as far as their consensus of perceived reality —the situational frames of reference by which we clothe perception with meaning and affect. The relative environmental statics for each of us seems to be the amended situational gestalts present in the nets and circuits of the cerebral cortex. It must be kept in mind that there also appears to be strong resistance to change both in our established overt and covert behavior. The amendments may be hypothesized to be the minimum necessary for testing reality and acceptable new perceptions and feedbacks. Most of us do believe that the automobile and the telephone are here to stay, but some of us are still somewhat unwilling to believe this of television and the digital computer.

These amended perceptions, the framework for which was set rather firmly in our youth, comprise the general settings of our environmental statics. Included as important categories of these statics are religion, geographical stampings, familial and neighborhood attitudes and beliefs, crisis periods such as serious long-term illness, military service, marital relationships, occupational aspirations and self-concepts of success or failure, rural versus urban origins, formal education, political affiliations and exposures, persistent self-images, and a host of other relevant conditioners of people.

When the statics of environment are interpreted against the personality statics of individuals and the degree of integration or consonance of the two can be studied by the client and the psychologist, we may then be much better prepared to plunge into what we hope is a projection of these joint statics into sound dynamics for planning.

DYNAMICS

What man has been, he will tend to be. The environments of yesterday and tomorrow will yield often distorted, but recognizable, reflections of each other. The discussions which have preceded this section have established artificial, but perhaps helpful, dichotomies labeled the statics of personality and the statics of environment. A more accurate analogy is, of course, that of the biologist, physiologist, or surgeon working with the veins, arteries, and nerve fibres in living tissue. Some, or all, of the interacting disappears if we eliminate the dynamics of life in any one of the systems.

Chapter 3 dealt with some of the contributors to the dynamics of human personality operating in an environment. We have looked briefly at the dynamics of the social environment of which the individual human personality is a part. Social environment is composed of interacting human personalities. And change is dynamics. Learning theory and personality theory, perhaps opposite sides of a single coin, have yielded hypotheses from which we can further hypothesize about the interactions of being.

It is at this juncture that the psychologist enters most meaningfully into relationships with the client through which he hopes to bring realization of some of the objectives of the relationship. As has been seen in earlier chapters, the traits, motivations, goals, and learning potentials and structures of the client, clarified and investigated jointly by the two participants in process, can be structured into a coherent whole. Recapitulating, the psychologist will tend to adhere to hypotheses and theories with some elements of uniqueness—no one knows *the* structure.

The reader will find a selection of structures discussed in Chapters 2 and 3. Hypotheses of various researchers and writers are presented relative to needs, self-actualization, temperaments, interest patterns, occupational-personality dimension relationships, goals, and motivations. We refrain from recommending here any particular structure which we might judge to have general application for all, or most, clients or psychologists. Tentative suggestion for such a structure is planned for Volume 2.

Assuming that the client and the psychologist are in some agreement or, at least, that the client has reinforced some of his original concepts of himself in his environment, as modified by communication with the psychologist, we move toward the final step in process in terms of the present series of interchanges—that of client planning.

CLIENT PLANNING

Our clients spread over an age range of approximately thirty or forty years—from thirty to sixty, or more. Some are in the early stages of being with elements of becoming still in the picture. Certain felt needs of these clients often will include acquiring the necessary status symbols for highly self-actualized being. Let us take for our example the status of organizations such as the service clubs. Whether or not the personality dynamics of the younger client include a strong need for belonging and interacting in such settings, he may believe, correctly, that status progress is more rapid with the "proper" affiliations. The rewards of membership can be, for him, almost completely divorced from good fellowship and a desire to do good for humanity. In fact, his objectives may be "to do humanity good." If the older client is well established as being, he may still be a sound member of the organization, but he has passed, or is passing, through the chain of offices. The rewards and goals have changed and, for many, are still changing. Power and prestige needs are being met. If our client is moving into the setting of having been, he may feel a bit put-upon as younger members follow in his footsteps, but often he is most happy to have others take over the time-consuming details. The meetings become places for seeing old friends and believing that the environment is indeed comfortingly stable. Goals and motivations are still changing, however; and the need for alternative behaviors may be felt. If the activity is dropped, and there are not other actions or plans to replace it, degrees of freedom have been lost.

Our first example was one of middle- or upper-middle class membership. Examples in the lower-middle class include the individual who has been a skilled workman with concrete objects in three-dimensional space. Super (1940) has indicated that he is most likely to seek hobbies and, by inference, retirement activities related to his occupation. Should he, for example, become enamored with miniature trains, their construction, maintenance, and operation, it is probable that finances will place limitations on the scope of the hobby. He may well turn to a group venture which will share the costs and, as a side or main value, include social aspects.

In both of the examples above, although drawn from different socioeconomic levels, there was an activity in which intrinsic rewards were present in a marked degree. Crook and Heinstein

(1958), in a study of the attitudes of industrial workers toward aging and retirement, report discouragingly little planning by members of their sample. Here we have individuals in activities where the satisfactions of life come, not from the job, but from factors extrinsic to job satisfaction. There is no conclusive evidence, but many arrows indicate that significant self-actualization is correlated with personality dimensions limited to much less than 100 per cent of the population. The socioeconomic pressures and conditions appear to place much greater restrictions on the possibilities for increasing degrees-of-choice-freedom where the urban industrial worker is concerned.

Moving from specific situations to generalizations, the client and the psychologist are attacking the problems of fitting self-images to perceived situations and fields and, in a sense, performing the kind of matching which characterizes counseling psychology and assessment with younger, becoming, clients. What kinds, and how many, alternatives or degrees of freedom can be found and considered by the client?

The answer to the questions regarding a client's capacity for knowing about, or acting on, possible alternatives lies in both the resources of the individual and the opportunities afforded by the immediate environment. The reader is referred back to the materials concerning self-actualization in Chapter 4. The criterion of degree of self-actualization tends to be the self-image of the client, not the potentialities inferred by peers or the opinion of experts, i.e., psychologists. Each of us will make our decisions in terms of our perceived wants, needs, and interests. These in turn will be modified by our available energy, the opportunities we know about and which are at hand, and the limitations of finances, family responsibilities, backgrounds, and other factors.

It is a fairly safe assumption that all alternatives of some promise will not be obvious to either the client or the psychologist alone. Interaction, particularly as there is discussion by the client of his world, should produce new alternatives in addition to the combinations and syntheses of the more obvious ones. If bibliocommunication is carefully organized, the client has an additional source of relevant information. In the self-matching of the client to alternatives, there is an excellent chance that better behavior, in client terms, will result.

THE PSYCHOLOGIST AND CLIENT PLANNING

Figure 2, based on concepts developed by Pepinsky (1952) and Bordin (1946), indicates some of the directions in which the psychologist's contribution tends to go. Ethics and wisdom both indicate the need for the psychologist to accept clients only after an adequate medical examination. It is assumed that limiting conditions of health, such as diabetes, arthritis, heart conditions, and arrested tuberculosis, are known to the psychologist as well as any deformities which have physical or psychological implications for client planning. Particularly when the client choices lie in hobby and avocational fields, there is need for knowledge of health hazards surrounding them.

Although any of Pepinsky's categories, at the extremes, could indicate conditions where psychotherapy might be in order, some of the conditions—choice-anxiety, lack of assurance, lack of information, and lack of skill—tend to be conditions faced and coped with often by the client. Dependence, cultural self-conflict, interpersonal self-conflict, and intrapersonal self-conflict seem to be more frequently associated with patients and psychotherapy although, in many instances, there are evidences of their presence in clients.

The reader will note that some of the conditions, and all of the problem contexts, call for psychologist competence in the skills of *assessment*. The objectives, however, include these assessment data in the molar psychoevaluation. Should the psychologist have reason to believe that psychotherapy should precede, or accompany, psychoevaluation, he will frequently refer to a psychotherapist, unless he is one of the relatively few psychologists who has competence to carry on both processes himself.

Use of the twofold figure permits the psychologist to plot the

Figure 2 Assessment and Evaluation Context

Conditions affecting adaptation, distribution, and adjustment	*Other areas of concern*	*Social participation (preference behavior)*	*Philosophy of life (values and goals)*	*Aptitudes, abilities, interests*	*Self-actualization*	*Understanding of environment*	*Understanding of self*
Normality indicators: Choice-anxiety							
Lack of assurance							
Lack of information							
Lack of skill							
Psychotherapy indicators: Dependence							
Cultural self-conflict							
Interpersonal self-conflict							
Intrapersonal self-conflict							
Other conditions							

patterns in a manner which indicates the major directions for structuring. Placing the number "1" in each cell which represents appreciable client difficulty, a "2" in those which are of importance, and a "3" in cells where some consideration may be needed, enables us to arrive at a case summary. If the number "1" appears concentrated in the group of conditions labeled "Psychotherapy," the kind of communication with the client may be planned in a different way than would be the case if the pattern concentrated in the section of "Normality indicators."

However, the major burdens of both the client and the psychologist in psychoevaluation must be carried through communication. A separate chapter is devoted to the implementation of process through communication.

Chapter 7

COMMUNICATION

TO A GREATER extent than is found in psychotherapy or counseling psychology, written communication can carry a major load in psychoevaluation. In psychotherapy, particularly of the non-directive type, the content of therapist speech is frequently of less import than the reflection of feelings and emotions. In counseling, which places a major burden on assessment, there is need for terminology that can be understood by the client; but because we assess against quite specific criteria, it is not essential that the cerebrations of the psychologist regarding these criteria be communicated in toto. Nor are the technicalities of assessment of usual importance to the client. In both psychotherapy and counseling, the "to" and "for" often outweigh the "with." The common ground with traditional medical practice and the necessary dependence of patients on the physician as "the knower" is clear.

Psychoevaluation requires that the psychologist give information and structure to the client in language which is, or easily becomes, part of the speech and thinking of the client. One example we can take from materials used in vocational counseling. The Minnesota occupational rating scales (Paterson, Gerken, Hahn, 1953) is based on seven terms found in the vocabulary of most clients. These are *academic, mechanical, social, clerical, musical, artistic,* and *physical agility.* These are contained in a two-dimensional structure of *field* and *level* (Hahn and Brayfield, 1945; Hahn and MacLean, 1955, 49–51). Communication is possible in these terms with many junior and senior high school students.

The reader will recognize, for example, that behind the word *academic* lies much research relative to human intelligence including the literature which is reflected in Buros's *Mental Measurements Yearbook.* Similar, but less impressive, masses of information and research buttress each of the other trait terms—mechanical, social, clerical, musical, artistic, and physical agility. The psychologist is expected to feel at home with these materials. But it is sometimes necessary that the client understand a generalized distillation of the pertinent literature and that he gain insight into his own perceptions as they are being clarified and perhaps changed by experience.

In dealing with this problem in Chapters 2 and 3, attention was called to the need to interpret findings, such as Cattell's (1957) *Universal Indices,* into verbalizations comprehendable by the client. Holland's (1962) approach to this is also pertinent. This interpretation of complex concepts into simpler language unquestionably brings about some dilution of the original meanings. However, meanings for the psychologist do not always coincide with meanings for the client. The problem of the psychologist is to hold dilution of relevant concept and construct purity to a minimum, at the same time that client comprehension is held to a maximum. There appears to be no alternative in professional psychology. We often cannot work with the client at the researcher's level or with the researcher at our client's level.

But the communication is a two-way street. The client has self-images which, while usually lacking in system, are strongly held and resistant to even semantic shifts. For the psychologist to achieve sound relationship, there is need for him to understand, translate, and interpret client self-concepts and environmental perceptions into a mutually derived set of communication symbols, verbal and nonverbal. Without this communication reciprocity, a process which is primarily cognitive can have rough sailing. With this brief look at the symbolic communication of expressive behavior and semantics, let us turn now to other considerations pertaining to communication. The reader who wishes to pursue the matter further will find entry to an interesting literature in Brown (1958), Piaget (1958), Korzybski (1951), and Hayakawa (1943).

Despite a highly flexible and quite formidable armamentorium of communication weapons, we seem to have placed our psychological eggs in the basket of the interview. Although the research affords a dismal view of the interview in terms of statistical reliability and validity of claimed outcomes, we seem stubbornly to refuse a look in other more promising directions under appropriate circumstances (Kelly and Fiske, 1950). Our possibilities include (1) *the interview,* (2) *records,* (3) *personal documents,* (4) *bibliocommunication,* (5) *nonverbal communication,* and (6) *psychologist's reports.*

The more obvious objectives, or purposes, for communication we take from Pepinsky (1948). Although his research was done with university undergraduates, his categories are valuable with other populations. These are (1) choice-anxiety, (2) lack of information, (3) lack of assurance, and (4) lack of skills. Some discussion of these conditions was presented in the preceding chapter; it is amplified here in more specific settings. One of the enigmas of professional psychology is the ability to produce seemingly excellent assessments, evaluations, and diagnoses, but seldom to match these with specific methodological proposals for client change through learning theory. Hypothetical though the following proposals may be, attempts will be made on the following pages to be somewhat specific in this area of communication prescription.

Choice-anxiety

Pepinsky (1952, 105) tends to place choice-anxiety close to his category of self-conflict. Although we are not in disagreement with his placement, there do appear to be situations where the distance between the categories increases markedly. The point is made because the writer includes choice-anxiety among the normality indicators and self-conflict with the psychotherapeutic indicators. The severity of either condition as it affects the client's problems of adaptation or adjustment would, of course, govern in most instances. Of choice-anxiety Pepinsky (1948, 105) says:

> The client who has *Choice-Anxiety,* like the *Self-Conflict* client, has a problem which constitutes a threat to his status and security. The decision which must be made is important to him and he is anxious because he cannot decide. As a result, the symptoms of *Choice-Anxiety* may be very similar to those of *Self-Conflict*—there will be evidences of emotional disturbance. Yet the client who has *Choice-Anxiety* will probably have little difficulty in stating his problem to the counselor, and the counselor will probably discover that this client has a rather clear notion of what his trouble is.

If the client and the psychologist are in agreement that a condition of choice-anxiety is present and of importance to the client, what do the two participants in the process do? It seems clear that until a choice is made, especially where either social or psychological survival is perceived by the client as threatened, there will tend to be a rising level of anxiety. Circumstances and the personality structure of the client will determine whether this anxiety remains at the irritating, interfering level or increases to where disintegrative aspects of adjustment appear. The psychologist must evaluate or diagnose the present level and probable course of the anxiety state. To himself he makes predictions. Having arrived at firm hypotheses for action, he must decide what combination of his communication skills will best fit the particular client and the situation in which he finds himself. In effect, the psychologist is perilously close to a prescription. And prescription in this sense is not necessarily a nasty word.

There are several obvious ingredients for a number of methodological prescriptions. These include advice, support, reflection of feeling, bibliocommunication, oral information giving, clarification and amplification of alternative actions through discussion, and the decision to use forcing methods (Hahn and MacLean, 1955,

261–264) with the client carrying the full load for the moment. It is certain that some combination of these ingredients will be structured and applied to the client through communication media. It is most difficult to imagine a client-psychologist relationship where prescription in this sense is not present.

Lack of Information

Pepinsky begins his description of the characteristics of this syndrome as follows: "If the *Lack-of-Information* syndrome is valid, we may generalize that clients in this category are maladjusted in that they possess insufficient or incorrect knowledge about themselves and/or the goals which they wish to achieve in life." What to do about it? The interview appears to be an ineffective and costly single method with which to help the client. Long lectures to an audience of one raise objections, even if the psychologist has the encyclopedic knowledge to undertake the task.

Personal documents by the psychologist, tailored to each client, do not appear reasonable in terms of time and predicted outcomes. This leaves us some form of bibliocommunication as one reasonable methodology by which to communicate. *Bibliocommunication* will be discussed at length later in this chapter. At this point we only wish to emphasize that in vocational counseling and guidance with clients in the period of becoming, the method has been moderately successful. With older clients there has been much less tendency to use the approach. The available material in the literature does not indicate conclusive research evidence pro or con. It seems reasonable to conclude that clients will seldom increase self-knowledge, and move toward a greater degree of self-actualization, without minimal relevant information in a number of directions and areas. Bibliocommunication as an adjunct to other information-providing techniques shows promise.

Lack of information can be approached by referral to specialists in pertinent areas. For example, if there is a desire on the part of a client to learn new skills of any complexity, we quite naturally use a referral to a competent authority. Lack of information can frequently be remedied by creating situations for and with the client in which he can make personal observations. This set of conditions is frequently met when information is desired regarding social or recreational outlets, new or different from the present activities. It is also encountered in the form of tours to the rapidly increasing number of special communities for various age or interest groups. Both method and content are flexible dimensions when working with clients who lack information.

Lack of Assurance

We may hypothesize that the *Lack of Assurance* client will, in general, have less disrupting adjustment problems than other clients. He is like the physically fit person who goes to a doctor to check on his health. Although goals of the *Lack of Assurance* client are appropriate, he does not feel competent to be his own judge; he therefore seeks expert opinion (Pepinsky, 1948, 72).

As is true of all of these four categories, the writer believes in this one that client problems of *adaptation* are of more importance than those of *adjustment.* Counseling psychologists in educational institutions often deal with lack of assurance by confirmation of choice. Stone (1948) has written an excellent description of the condition in college students. There is little need for advice or prescription when this condition is encountered. There are situations, of course, where supportive techniques are indicated. The client tends to have information and skills to make a decision but desires a bit more of reality testing. Choice-anxiety is not usually at a high level.

The interview frequently is the best method of dealing with lack of assurance. Clarification, support, and structuring are common, and often effective, psychologist contributions. There are many situations when self-study can be facilitated through bibliocommunication. Records and personal documents can be useful, and there are occasions when the psychologist's written reports will aid in both adaptation and adjustment. It is noted that lack of assurance, as is true of all the conditions discussed here, is latticed and enmeshed with cause, affect, and effect from the other category conditions.

Lack of Skills

This category, unlike the others although related to them, has to do with possible early sensory deprivation, environmental restrictions, and motivating factors which are highly internalized. For many clients the efficiency variables are crucial. It is most closely related to lack of information. Of this category Pepinsky says (1948, 80):

> The *Lack of Skill* client, then cannot reach desirable and otherwise appropriate goals because he has not learned to perform, adequately, certain requisite acts. His inadequate skill is apt to be a real handicap, since his competitors are able to do the same things with a facility and precision that leave him far behind. An important attribute of the *Lack of Skill* client is the counselor-judged appropriateness of his goals. Another is potential ability to reach them.

As stated above, Pepinsky did his research with college students, and so his statements regarding "counselor-judged appropriateness of his goals" and his "potential ability to reach them" are not of the same importance for older clients as they are for those between fifteen and twenty-five. We need to keep in focus the importance of the number and the quality of roles, as new roles can be learned and old ones polished or repaired (Sarbin, 1954). Other items of importance include not only the operational skills useful in productive and creative work but also the social skills which will aid in adaptation and environmental self-distribution. To some extent, self-sufficiency may be enhanced through consideration of its importance to certain clients. Our communication media can deemphasize some skill categories which are commonly awarded major emphasis, such as activity for the sake of activity, and transfer the energy to such vehicles as adult education, quasi apprenticeships, and home-study procedures. Social skills require a somewhat different grouping of communication resources, including social organizations sponsored by, and for, the age grouping of our clients. Nor should we ignore, for the group between forty and fifty-five, careful consideration of plans to acquire skills which would provide an appropriate level of stimulus and activity for the years after sixty-five.

In summary of Pepinsky's useful conditions of client ADAPTATION-Adjustment-distribution, it is noted that discussion has been limited to the more externalized conditions. The adjustment-loaded indicators—dependence, cultural self-conflict, interpersonal self-conflict, and intrapersonal self-conflict—have not been brought into sharp focus because they constitute material for another book if they are to receive the treatment they require. These indications are much more internalized and, in psychoevaluation, usually of less moment.

TOOLS AND TECHNIQUES OF COMMUNICATION

As was stated earlier, we have at least six major types of tools and techniques for communication between the client and the psychologist—the interview, records, personal documents, bibliocommunication, nonverbal communication, and psychologist's reports. In this section we are concerned with the considerations as to how these methodologies can best be used to aid the client in studying and understanding himself. Repeating again, our major concern is with client adaptation and self-distribution to, and within, cultures and subcultures. Adjustment variables are, of course, important but not major in this context.

Although no plane-surface, two-dimensional figure can present the complexities of the structure implied, and stated, in our discussion here, Figure 3 is included as a guide to the reader. Communication is more easily dealt with when the more relevant dimensions within which it is included are apparent. We now consider our methods of one-to-one communication in more detail.

THE INTERVIEW

Because the interview has been used in so many ways for so many purposes, no attempt is made to recommend a single publica-

Figure 3 Conditions, Situations, Understandings, and Communication Resources for Communication in Psychoevaluation

Conditions (Pepinsky)	Situations, younger clients (Williamson, Darley, Longstaff)	Understandings and insight, mature clients (Hahn)	Communication resources (Hahn)
Normality indicators:	Aptitudes and abilities	Understanding of self	The interview
Choice-anxiety	Educational planning	Aptitudes, abilities, interests	Records (including L, Q, and T test data)
Lack of information	Vocational planning	Understanding of environment	Personal documents (including autobiographies, letters, diaries, recordings)
Lack of assurance	Finances	Understanding of interaction dynamics	Bibliocommunication (including psychologist-originated materials)
Lack of skills	Social (general)	Self-actualization (social and self-criteria)	Nonverbal communication
Psychotherapy indicators:	Religious, moral, ethical	Philosophy of life (values and goals)	Psychologist's reports
Cultural self-conflict	Personality integration	Social participation (preferences-behavior)	
Interpersonal self-conflict	Emotional stability		
Intrapersonal self-conflict			
Dependence			

tion as encompassing all of its uses, objectives, and outcomes. The reader will find a reasonably good introduction to the topic from various viewpoints in Bingham, Moore, and Gustad (1959), Kahn and Cannell (1957), Hahn and MacLean (1955), Sullivan (1954), Darley (1941), and Symonds (1931).

Our consideration of the interview will not include its more specialized uses in industrial personnel work, psychotherapy, or counseling with younger clients, although the elements we consider important in psychoevaluation are found in all of these. These primary elements are *relationship, structure,* and *clarification.* It is recognized, of course, that under some circumstances with most clients imparting of information, support, and release of tension will take the center of the stage when appropriate. If the client is judged to have been poorly assessed or evaluated, a diagnosis has been missed, or there has been, or is occurring, a change of conditions during the client-psychologist relationship, the psychologist must "change his hat" and either enter into counseling or psychotherapy or refer the client to another practitioner deemed better qualified to counsel or treat. Should any of these contingencies arise, the objectives and structure of the interview will change along with the nature of the interviewing process.

Relationship

Some discussion of relationship was encountered in the preceding chapter. Here we reiterate that mutual respect and an absence of dislike are the minimal relationship requirements for client and psychologist. In that a stated condition in psychoevaluation is maximal client control of process and also of relationship structure, we proceed in ways different than when our roles center around to and for services. Although psychologist judgment will be followed in the selection of communication media, these selections must be acceptable to the client and in keeping with his broad personality pattern. In psychoevaluation many of the elements of the psychiatric interview are missing. Here there is no psychologist compulsion to cure an illness or radically to change personality dimensions or behaviors. Particularly, there should be avoidance of many of the sometimes punishing behaviors of the psychotherapeutic interview. Forcing to obtain client movement has little place with the normal, mature, self-actualizing individual.

Clients and psychologists deal with finite time. For many clients personal finances also have limits. Both of these considerations raise ethical problems regarding the period needed, or used, to establish relationship at a reasonable level. Because roles, not masks, are in clearest focus, relationship in psychoevaluation is not less important but of a different nature than in psychotherapy. In the interests of adequate process movement the psychologist must not only maintain relationship, but also provide, but not pedantically impose, interview structure. It should be kept in mind that planned lack of structure can be a rigid and authoritarian structure. Unplanned lack of structure can easily result in chaos and frustration for both the client and the psychologist.

In Chapter 1 the objectives of psychoevaluation were stated as client self-understanding, deeper client environmental insights, integration of self- and environmental understandings and insights, personal satisfactions and happiness, saving of client time, and more efficient use of social institutions. We are concerned with movement toward these objectives in any order which comes closest to being logically and psychologically sound. The client's needs and expectations and the situation as the psychologist perceives it are of importance to order and movement.

While it has been stated on the one hand that communication should facilitate client progress, it has, on the other hand, been stated that we will place a lighter load on the interview to obtain this progress. Communication and interview are not synonymous. The psychologist is concerned with an appropriate pattern for all methods of communication, and the use of the interview should contribute to the broad, general plan of process. There is no intent to imply that interviews should be controlled to the extent that planning would involve a minute-by-minute program comparable to the production of a show for radio or television. Structure must be far more flexible than that. On the other hand, as psychologist judgments of progress are continually reevaluated, the interview planning must attempt optimal process movement.

Reemphasis is given to the number of interviews judged necessary to carry the process to completion. The psychologist who uses all of the forms of communication in appropriate pattern should not need more than from five to ten 1-hour interviews with the client. The spacing of these interviews may extend calendar time to about three months, although the process for many clients will be appreciably less than this. If the interview schedule runs much beyond ten hours, there should be a growing suspicion on the part of the psychologist that he is dealing with ADJUSTMENT-Adaptation-distribution patterns, not ADAPTATION-Distribution-adjustment. If this be his conclusion, then of course process and communication forms and patterns should be recast to those appropriate to psychotherapy.

Clarification

Clarification concerns the content of the interview. Much that is pertinent here will be encountered also in the section labeled *bibliocommunication*. Because of this, we consider at this point the more generalized aspects of clarification. The professional psychologist is a relative newcomer compared to the physician or lawyer. In addition, because there are several breeds of professional psychologists, the client may not be certain either as to his own role or that of the psychologist. Perhaps the modal percept of the psychologist to the American public is that of a "headshrinker"—a kind of psychiatrist. A first concern, therefore, is to clarify the client-psychologist roles. This is usually attempted through the use of the interview alone. However, many of us have been astonished and dismayed at the perceptions some of our clients demonstrate regarding our functions, sometimes after several interviews.

Let us suppose that in line with the discussion of bibliocommunication, the client, before or during a first interview, receives a dignified, personalized description of the relationship in written form. While in this early interview, there will be discussion of the what, why, and how of the processes and roles involved the major focus will be that of establishing relationship. Because of this emphasis, the conversation content may not have the impact for learning that the psychologist intends. The use of the printed statement of relationship for reference during a first interview may be helpful for clients. If the client reads the materials after the first but before subsequent meetings, he will have questions which lend themselves to the objectives of clarification. The written materials often help to structure future interview content in desired directions, thus facilitating process. It is hoped that more informed questions by the client, in terms of greater insight and information, will enable the client and the psychologist to move toward process objectives with greater sureness and speed.

A second area of interview content and clarification is that having to do with the nomothetic aspects of assessment and psychoevaluation. If the client is to study himself to greatest personal benefit, in what semantic framework is the study and its attendant interview communication to be conducted? Here again it is possible to use bibliocommunication as an adjunct to the interview. While the content of interviews will deal with personality development and dimensions, feelings, attitudes, values, goals, specific informations, and related matters, there must be jointly understood verbal symbols and concepts for the communication.

A third important consideration in clarification is the interview exchange regarding the client's tentative hypotheses and understandings in his self-culture images. The psychologist will be formulating, amplifying, and discarding hypotheses about the client as the process proceeds. He must shape his communications to meet these tentative hypotheses, evaluating the relative importance of client lack of information, lack of skill, lack of assurance, and choice-anxiety. As hypotheses become more firm, clarification with the client will follow the jointly indicated directions in the interview. So long as psychologist hypotheses are not perceived by the client as judgmental, authoritarian, or pedantic, they are legitimate matters for interview content. The client is still in general control, and the psychologist is working with him.

In summary of the interview as one method of client-psychologist communication, we reiterate our outcome aims for its use. If it is a successful method of communication, it will be a major factor in the establishment of rapport. It will facilitate the origination, exchange, and clarification of concepts. Reality testing will be made easier for the client through feedback in a nonjudgmental setting. There will be elements of support at certain points and in some situations, although seldom will this support be in the form of pure reflection of feelings. Above all, the interview will tend to be the integrating factor for all of the other methods of communication, but when this is said, we still assign to it a far less backbreaking load than has been our wont in the past. Our attention is now directed to a second form of client-psychologist communication—*personal records.*

PERSONAL RECORDS AS COMMUNICATION

With records, as with other forms of communication, it is necessary with mature clients to utilize them to contribute to client self-study. There is little need to comment on the usual population data which are collected for identification and psychologist information regarding educational, vocational, familial, and social backgrounds. Forms for the collection of such information are so familiar to the reader that no further mention is needed here.

Records can be used for purposes other than converting dynamics into statics for future reference. They obviously serve multiple objectives. Figure 4 is offered as an example of this. For one purpose, we obtain a record of the client's activity style as he has perceived it at various checkpoints in his life history. We ask him to bring the activity record down to the present and then to project it into a period ahead. Through this device we also can supply information of the wide range of activities open to people. Through a multiple-purpose record of this kind, the client may perceive a loss of degrees-of-choice-freedom in the activity area which because it is disturbing to him will open alternative behaviors which are

Figure 4 Activity Preferences and Behaviors

Activities:	*Before age 25*			*Age 26 to 35*			*Age 36 to 45*			*Present decade*			*Next decade*		
	YES	*Yes*	*NO*	*YES*	*Yes*	*NO*	*YES*	*Yes*	*NO*	*YES*	*Yes*	*NO*	*YES*	*Yes*	*NO*
Archery															
Bicycling															
Choir work															
Collecting plants															
Cooking															
Fishing															
Folk or square dancing															
Gardening															
Member social club															
Playing bridge															
Reading aloud to others															
Sculpture															
Stamp or coin collecting															
Woodworking															

more satisfying. Insights may be acquired into a crucial expansion-contraction, activity-dormancy condition.

When psychometric devices are used, the scores, and even particular item responses, may provide materials for communication relevant to the client and process movement. The patterns of test and inventory scores provide the psychologist with information which can be helpful in communication. Although, as Cattell (1957, 45–73) has indicated, the collection of meaningful life-record data is difficult, the difficulties of interpretation of these data are even greater. Here again there is a severe test of the psychologist's communication skills. If we consider the client and the psychologist as message originators and decoders in a two-way communication net, both social sensitivity and communication skills are involved in judgments concerning the wavelengths and qualitative dimensions of the receiving equipment.

Our records of clients will not usually be formal in nature. Personal documents must be used frequently in lieu of data available in other forms for younger people. A question which bears on the life history and other autobiographical material is that of how well the present status meets the predictions made earlier in his life. If we have confidence in the reliability of certain interest inventories and scales of values over a long time period, we can, in a sense, move backward in time and compare history and life-style with what the inventory discloses now. Career data are often revealing in evaluating personality dimensions. The story of earlier life stages may have an important bearing on our process, but the data for this story must be found in records quite different from those available for a high school or college student.

PERSONAL DOCUMENTS

In the preceding section the use of a personal document as a record was discussed. Although mention of personal documents as data for professional psychologists is frequent in the literature, they have not been used as widely as other sources of client-psychologist communication. Familiar references include Gordon Allport (1942) and the related work of Charlotte Buhler (1935). Of interest too is the research of Madorah Smith (1952) in her analysis of the language behavior of a single adult subject over a period of fifty years. Smith's data came from letters written by the subject and categorized in part by the decades of increasing age from forty-nine to eighty-nine.

The place of personal documents in professional psychology can be encapsulated as "iffy." Merited criticism has been leveled at them in terms of reliability and validity. Under certain circumstances one must agree with Guilford (1959, 324) when he says: "The study of a product is about as complex a task as the study of a person himself, and being once removed from the person, the product is likely to be of considerably less value than the person himself as an object of study."

However, in situations where a major concern is the study of an individual by himself, reliability and validity in the ordinary sense may not be important. It is difficult to conceive of a general pattern of conscious self-deception in writing. Insofar as Guilford's criticism is concerned, under the circumstances which we are considering, it is likely to be no more time-consuming and no more valueless than many of the methods employed routinely where we do use "the person himself as an object of study." Certainly the interview has demonstrated no great validity or reliability as a method of study. With younger subjects tests have done quite well in this regard, but what tests do we use with normal, mature, self-actualizing individuals?

But it is not our purpose here to enter a detailed discussion of personal documents. All that is intended is to present them as methods of client-psychologist communication hypothetically useful under some conditions. The specific instruments which appear to have usefulness in psychoevaluation are the autobiography, the life history, letters, and the transcribed tape recording.

The Autobiography

The most extensive use of the autobiography appears to be in formal education, particularly in the guidance programs of secondary education. Materials on such use will be found in sources such as Cottle and Downie (1960) and Hahn and MacLean (1955). Some use is found also in attitude research, such as that of Stouffer (1931). What is proposed here is the use of the autobiography as a substitute for what has too often ineffectively been done in the interview.

A common form is the life history, where the client attempts the ambitious project of writing an extensive chronological life story. Because this approach is of some magnitude for many clients, there is more often recourse to special areas of the history. What these areas are depends on the psychologist's judgment of the most appropriate material and the client's seemingly pressing anxieties.

If self-images are relevant, many clients are willing to write about "What I think I am like," "How other people see me," "What I would like to be like." If comparisons among and between these topics are desired, all of them may be included in a single presentation. If the focus of attention is planning ahead, topics can be used, such as "Pressure points that have shaped my career," "New Year's resolutions for the next decade," or "Changes I would like to make in my environment." These examples afford a brief view of the flexibility of this communication form. The chief value is, of course, giving the client focal points of attention from which greater personal insight may be possible. The autobiography also lends itself well for interview content.

The mature, normal, self-actualizing individual is frequently a busy person. Appointments are likely to suffer as the client perceives more important uses for the scheduled time or is resistant to the structure of process. It has been interesting, in my personal experience, to note the willingness to write a letter as a substitute for an interview which has been missed. When a client is travelling for an extended period, the correspondence may indicate that he is "working" on the process even though physical meetings with the psychologist are, for the time being, interrupted. This is not to be construed as encouraging practice by mail! It is possible to utilize some correspondence to facilitate psychoevaluation under some circumstances.

The autobiography and the letter can take some pressure off of the interview. If used, they also force the psychologist to a different set of duties. "Homework" assumes greater importance. Impact of communication is lost if the client must repeat in the interview materials which he has made available to the psychologist in written form. There is need for close professional attention to such communication, more conscientious attention than we sometimes give to our records prior to our interview sessions.

The Transcribed Tape Recording

Tape recordings of interviews have been used for a long period of time both as communications research material and for the instruction of graduate students. Greenwald, in his book *Call Girl,* gives another illustration of its use in psychotherapy. Patients, or givers of information relevant to the study, in some instances refused to meet him face to face. Some of them were willing "to interview" him via tape recorder. The transcription appeared at times even more revealing than the interview. However, with our normal client we seldom will encounter situations which bring about a refusal to see us personally. There will be conditions in which the client may feel that he has important material and would like to talk with us, but no appointment is possible at the time and the recording is substituted. There are also the occasions when travel or illness prevents interviews at a time when the client is motivated toward process movement. The advantages in these circumstances are obvious. The recording, if listened to in its entirety by the psychologist, has one disadvantage—it takes hour for hour with the client, even though the psychologist has more freedom in choosing a convenient time to listen. Many of us prefer to have a typed transcript and to treat this in much the same manner as we would other written autobiographical material. Where psychotherapy is involved, both listening and transcribing appear to have desirable features.

The personal documents may serve as a major agent in building client self-assurance. Structuring the content of the document can aid the client in this direction. Personal documents may be of help in the conditions of lack of information and lack of skill. If the client perceives himself as lacking in either respect, he may be motivated to do a bit of investigation in the effort to obtain a decrease of tensions and to satisfy the urges toward exploration. Clarification of issues usually contributes some alleviation of choice-anxiety because of the effects of more information, skill, assurance, and better reality testing. Personal documents merit consideration in psychoevaluation and its needs for communication which in many instances are not met by the interview alone.

NONVERBAL COMMUNICATION

There has been a growing interest in communication theory and research regarding it in the technical fields surrounding automation and the use of electronic devices which have demanded more rapid and accurate sending and decoding devices. Final interpretation of communication has tended to remain in the province of man, not machine. In large part because the demand for speed and accuracy of communication has not caused heavy pressures on "talking doctors," there has been less movement in the professional fields of working with problems of adaptation, distribution, and adjustment. Ruesch and Kees (1960) and Morrison (1961) afford insight into the limited materials available which are directed at face-to-face communication through motor activities, gestures, postures, and facial expressions. This section is devoted to observations and hypotheses regarding the "vocabulary" of nonverbal communication.

The first consideration is to the *surround* in the restricted sense of the physical settings including persons, but not the interactions among and between people. These interactions, following English and English (1958) are considered as components of situations. If an individual arranges a place for work as he or she wishes it to be, inspection of the final result should permit reasonably valid inferences regarding some personality dimensions of that individual. Color, light, size, shape, type of furnishings, placement of objects and people—all of these contribute to a surround "personality" which conveys impressions and meaning to the occupant and his callers. Even with modern decor and design, a bank is seldom confused with a rathskeller or a police station with a beauty salon.

One can "impress" others; place them at advantages or disadvantages; make them comfortable or uncomfortable, warm or cold, irritated or calm by the handling of the surround. There may well be nonverbal communication of greater or lesser moment when a client steps into the psychologist's office. With unknown validity the caller may perceive the occupant as prissy, careless, stuffy, careful, relaxed, friendly, or cold in terms of the professional surround.

The implications of professional role playing are many. We see the caricatured general impressions of occupational stereotypes in the delightful eighteenth and nineteenth century cartoons of, for example, lawyers and physicians. Psychologists have not as yet acquired a public image as clear as that of older professions, but each psychologist plays a role with clients and patients in terms of his own images of the psychologist in action. And nonverbal role playing is an important medium of communication. We do clothe our role playing with a patter of words. If the words and the role behavior are perceived as consistent, we may be considered as sincere. If there is divergence between the two, insincerity is a more probable label.

Movement toward or away from individuals may communicate with great clarity. One may speculate that these perceptions are genetic and remnants of primitive, biological survival behaviors. "If it runs, chase it. It thinks you can eat it. If it runs at you, run away. It thinks it can eat you." Regardless of the speculation, whatever the principles which underly our reactions in these situations, they have been made use of by organizations which distribute products door to door. Manuals have been written for salesmen which instruct them to step back (run) when the housewife comes to the door. She will more often than chance open the door (chase). The second move is to proffer a small gift the acceptance of which requires the further opening of the door. Sales figures indicated that the behaviors worked, particularly when accompanied by oral patter carefully tested and learned by rote. In more subtle manners, professional service workers utilize these and many other generalized nonverbal behaviors for purposes of communication.

It is obvious that we can seldom separate the more gross bodily cues, gestures, facial expressions, and eye fixations and movements. For this discussion it may appear to the reader that the author is attempting such a task. The intention is to discuss various aspects of nonverbal communication as if they were discrete but to keep in mind that several, or all, of the kinds of cues are being used in the professional role at the same time.

These gross bodily postures carry over into communication of psychologist attitudes and concerns. "I am attending," "I am interested," "What you are saying is important"—these statements are at least as often conveyed by the maintenance of some observable bodily tension and physical orientation *toward* the client or patient as by making the statements. If the bodily tensions are relaxed and the orientation is *away* from the client, unless eye fixation is used to counteract the posture, one is frequently perceived as saying, "I am not attending," "This is boring or irrelevant," "Go away." Both the quantity of the client's oral output and its direction are under some psychologist control without verbal cues.

It is possible to categorize broad types of bodily movement or statics in terms of intended or unintended communication. As examples we choose the *Christ of the Andes* figure and *foetal positions.* The open-armed, "come unto me," warm, expansive feeling tone of the former is well understood in our culture. Observation of professional practitioners in psychology and related disciplines indicates a common knowledge and acceptance of these bodily sets and gestures as "common words" in the nonverbal vocabulary. The foetal image is much more often unconsciously used and is frequently more a revelation of the personality dimensions of the user than a conscious attempt to communicate feelings and attitudes. The tight, in-the-womb, self-protective, rejective impression on observers is not always unnoticed.

Gestures, like languages, are often directly related to cultures or subcultures. Few have universal meaning. Even the headshaking approvals and negations reverse their meanings from one setting to another. It is probable that a full-scale investigation of our cultural gesture vocabulary would reveal an astonishingly large number of communication symbols. The raised, closed fist; the pounding of shoes in the United Nations; the thumb to nose with fingers extended; the throat cutting with a finger as a symbolic knife; the sign language of workers in motion pictures, radio, and television—these are but samples of the common cultural gesture language. Professional providers of services to others combine numerous gestures, bodily postures, and eye fixations with facial expressions and physical surrounds for rich communication, some of which cannot be duplicated by the spoken or written word.

Eye fixations appear also to contribute greatly to nonverbal communication. In literature throughout its history the references to the eye as an index of the individual personality are numerous and universal. Many professional boxers profess to read an opponent's intended moves by watching his eyes. We find such expressions as, "I don't trust that man. He never smiles with his eyes." This is interesting but is used here only to point up the importance to communication of eye movement and fixation on the part of the psychologist. It is still surprising to the writer to encounter so many graduate students in professional psychology who do not know where to look during a conversation. Although popular novels have their lovers "gazing into her eyes," this is an almost impossible physical feat. We really "gaze into her *eye*." Observation indicates that we make others comfortable in conversation when we select one eye at a time, fixate for ten to twenty seconds, and then shift to the other. Gaze at the hairline and noticeable anxiety appears. Lock gazes and we express hostility and intended aggression. Refuse to attend to the eye fixation during a conversation and we convey a number of possible "decodings" including evasion, shame, guilt, disinterest, and aversion or active dislike. Eye use for communication is, of course, a part of facial expression, the next topic.

Facial expressions convey much of the nonverbal, face-to-face burden of communication. Although research has been done with content analysis of interviews, there is a suspicion that recordings have at times lost at least half of the communication which was taking place. Just as the recording has advantages over the typed transcription because inflections and intonations are essentials of oral communication, so does the observation of the interview situation or its motion picture reproduction have advantages over the recording. One can ask questions, supply assurance and support, reprimand, encourage, exhibit friendliness or enemity, approve, disapprove, reject, and accept all by use of the eyes, eyebrows, lips, and head movements. These localized behaviors fit into the total bodily communications which, in turn, buttress and clarify verbalizations. We communicate face to face with a complex interaction of communication components.

If the reader is involved in the training of professional psychologists, he can examine the nonverbal communications by having a graduate student well rehearsed on what is to be communicated in a scheduled interview. If at every possible point the communication content is then rehearsed with the substitution of nonverbal symbols for verbal symbols, the results can be surprising. A very simple exercise of this sort is to have a student greet a client at the office door, establish rapport, seat the client, make him comfortable, and then have the client begin the interview—all without a spoken word. It is not particularly difficult to do.

BIBLIOCOMMUNICATION

This topic reintroduces some of the considerations already presented in the discussion of the interview. Pepinsky's (1948) categories have raised the problems of effective communication with an optimal expenditure of client-psychologist time. Although there may be many psychologists who consistently use methods other than the interview for communicating about these conditions, they have not written widely on the subject. Nor have graduate training programs emphasized noninterview communication. Where problems center about *adjustment,* with adaptation and distribution in a minor role, in some situations we do utilize noninterview techniques, such as play therapy with children and role playing for older clients and patients. Also the guidance programs of secondary schools and colleges use printed occupational information and motion pictures to reduce interview time and convey information the details of which few psychologists have believed it necessary to learn.

English and English (1958) in their dictionary of psychological and psychoanalytical terms do not include *bibliocommunication.* They do include *bibliotherapy* and define it as "the utilization of reading for cure or amelioration of psychic disorder; more broadly, the use of reading to promote mental hygiene." Even though bibliocommunication is not included, there is a strong presumption that clients and patients are directed regularly to the literature for information deemed by the psychologist as pertinent and useful to aid people to better adaptation, adjustment, and distribution. The method is widely used in medicine; for example, the prenatal and postnatal monographs for parents and the practice of making selected items in medical journals available to some patients about ailments.

In the chapter on the client, space was devoted to problems in various age groups, particularly in the *being* and *having been* categories, partial solutions for which might be found by reading. Although there are carefully prepared and published lists of information about occupations, these seldom contain materials aimed at the self-actualizing adult. We have need for materials designed for these clients. Rather than provide even a short list of specific recommendations, we will consider here the major outlines of the method and the conditions of greatest frequency in the adult population.

There is always the danger that problems are being created in advocating greater emphasis on techniques which can be easily misused. An example is cogently presented by Ernest Havemann, in the August 8, 1960, issue of *Life.* Indiscriminate use of bibliotherapy and bibliocommunication without some personal responsibility, control, and *prescription* by a qualified professional worker may do at least as much harm as good. We present bibliocommunication as part of a highly personalized, face-to-face professional relationship between a client operating, in the main, at the cognitive level with emphasis on problems of adaptation and a psychologist qualified to work with such a client. The author claims little competence in the use of bibliotherapy or communication if serious problems of adjustment are involved. Let us then, within these limitations and with caution, consider some broad dimensions of bibliocommunication under the rubrics psychologist's professional materials, adult education, community resources for social, recreational, and avocational activities, and retirement planning.

Psychologist's Professional Materials

In Chapters 4 and 5 about clients, it has been stressed that individuals without an established need for psychotherapy, but with a strong desire for self-understanding, have difficulty in finding professional assistance. Some of the problem lies in lack of information about what kind of professional person is qualified to deal primarily with personal adaptation and distribution. Even when a client places himself in the hands of a psychologist, roles are not clear. There is no need to review here the well-established tendencies of the man or woman in our culture to perceive such situations, and relationships, selectively. It is doubtful that all clients can give a clear description of relationship to the psychologist after an hour devoted to establishing rapport and explaining the relationship. Even in situations where physicians deal with "experienced" patients, there are, according to their reports, ambiguities regarding relationship.

It is suggested that the psychologist will avoid some ambiguities and save interview time for himself and his client if dignified, ethical, client-language and perception-oriented monographs are available to the client at various stages of the psychoevaluation and assessment processes. One title is *The Process;* others are *Personality Structure, Matching People and Communities,* and *Being and Having Been.*

While materials like these have been, and are being, used, it appears that we can make a better professional effort both qualitatively and quantitatively. Mimeographed sheets do not always carry the same status messages as do printed materials on a good quality of paper. Roughly outlined ideas, however sound, are not reasonable facsimiles of thoughtfully prepared, personalized materials. One example of this approach, of course, is the psychologist's written report to the client at the conclusion of the process. The psychologist's written resume for the client is discussed in more detail in the final section devoted to communication. All the bibliocommunication materials and methods have one aspect in common—they provide content for interview discussions. If the clarifying aspect of the interview is not used in conjunction with the printed materials, it may be better if it is not used.

Adult Education

One of the rapidly growing and important efforts which has attained increasing stature in the United States in the past two decades is adult education. There are few locations in our more populous and industrialized states where the individual does not have access to these increasing opportunities in one form or another. However, there is sufficient evidence to indicate that the interested consumer must beware in making choices. Because many of the psychologist's clients will consider further formal or semiformal education of one kind or another, it is most helpful if materials describing the legitimate offerings be available to the psychologist and to the client.

With the bewildering individual differences which clients present, few of us are in a position to discuss specific opportunities without reference to the printed page. Furthermore, discussion of the pros and cons of community resources for adult education is not always the most fruitful manner in which to use the interview. The professional psychologist in practice with the problems of adaptation and distribution as his forte will need materials regarding the institutions which he can endorse after personal investigation. Included will be the extension offerings of local colleges and universities; special offerings of public schools, junior colleges, and private enterprises; and individuals offering specialized skill training. Many psychologists believe that they have an obligation to supply information and, in addition, to act as guarantors for the integrity of that information. When we deal with a problem of adjustment and obtain release from disruptive anxiety for the patient, we can part with him at the office door. When we deal with adaptation, assessment, and evaluation, we must go with the client out into the community, and our responsibility does not end until he is satisfied within reason.

Legitimate and Ethical Community Resources for Social, Recreational, and Avocational Opportunities

Any professional person who has worked with clients and patients in the age range from thirty upwards is aware of the similarities to the small child, held within the house by the weather, who plaintively and irritatingly intones, "What can I do now, M-o-o-t-h-e-r?" This is in line with Anderson's emphasis on the use of time. Gordon Allport (1958) has stated the matter well: "Existential psychology tells us that Western man, in freeing himself from the drive-pressures of hunger, disease and fatigue, has run headlong into a vacuum where boredom and meaninglessness usurp his being."

Leisure time is an attractive abstraction. But the moment we do something with it, it is no longer leisure time. There are few situations more trying to individuals in our culture than those with stimuli below the accustomed activity level. The protestant ethic, the "man in the gray flannel suit," an early environment characterized by multiple stimuli and responses peculiar to the West, and the socioeconomic scramble as we move from becoming onto the ladder of being—all appear to operate against an easy transition to having been. The reader may find a review of the material in Chapters 4 and 5 useful on these matters.

The psychologist concerned with these transitional problems assumes a responsibility of some weight in terms of understanding and making available to clients the social, recreational, and avocational resources of the community and region. The dynamics must be inferred from a bewildering welter of statics. We have organizations of all sizes, shapes, and goals—private enterprise; government; educational institutions, public and private; business and industry; and religion—each attempting to meet human wants and needs. The needs are relatively few in number but the wants are without limit, and it is to the wants that entrepreneurs and bureaucrats are reputed to address themselves.

Again, the psychologist is ethically responsible for personal investigation of resources to which he may direct a client, either by a general recommendation or a specific reference. It is not enough to say, "You should investigate clubs which are organized to . . . ." Clients are not generally expert in making judgments, legal or otherwise, in a jungle of dollar competition in an unfamiliar setting. Nor, without personal investigation and continuing follow-up, can the psychologist say, "The Etoinshrdlu Association operates in this field. Why don't you inquire about it?"

It is strongly recommended that the psychologist gather information about resources, investigate for purposes of evaluation, organize a system for periodic reinvestigation, and make certain that what is called to the attention of clients represents sound professional judgment. There are legal implications for the private practitioner which cannot be ignored if he wishes to remain financially and professionally solvent. This matter of matching clients to use of leisure time also has been discussed on other pages.

Because the psychologist cannot be expected to carry all of this information in his head or take up interview time with prospectuses, bibliocommunication should carry much of this content. To some practitioners there is merit in preparing appropriate materials for their clients by evaluating and providing printed or duplicated documents. There is always the convenience of using printed materials prepared by the organization or enterprise when, in the psychologist's judgment, they are of a type which will be helpful to interested clients. The availability of these materials to clients should facilitate psychoevaluation.

Retirement Planning

Whether retirement planning "belongs" to gerontology, to the psychological specialist with the normal, or to the psychotherapist is an unsettled question. However, depending on many circumstances, psychologists from all three special areas do deal with the problems and the clients. The author is not familiar with definitive published materials in this regard which are of universal appeal or application. Materials of specific application to retirement planning, pointed to help with the matching of the individual to the more appropriate of many possible situations, remain to be written. In the series of which this book is a part, such published information is planned. Present practice appears to be to place the greatest burden of communication on the interview. Assessment must play a part, geography and climate cannot be ignored, medical facilities may be important, as are a number of other variables patterned to the needs and wants of the particular client.

If the planning is with a psychologist in private practice, one type of structure will appear. If the psychologist is employed by an industrial or governmental institution, another pattern of policy and practice may be indicated. If the service is provided by a social agency, such as a university facility, still different policies may be in evidence. There is a strong rationale for professional retirement advisement and communication for our senior citizens regardless of the degree of self-actualization judged to be present in the individual. The more printed material of high quality which is made available, the better the psychologist can meet his social and professional obligations.

Summarizing Bibliocommunication

In the past several pages we have seen a generalized approach to providing clients who lack information, skill, and assurance with information which supplements what can be done in interview situations. Descriptions have been provided regarding the nature of printed materials which were of help in some situations and under stated conditions. It was made clear that much of what is needed has not been written in appropriate form for use with clients. Emphasis has been given to the psychologist's ethical and legal responsibilities for the accuracy and integrity of information contained in bibliocommunication media. The bias of the author has been that no psychologist of his acquaintance has all, or most, of the possible important minutiae of specifics that practice with normal people demands. Bibliocommunication has been presented as a process which is in need of more systematic approaches, better quality, and research attention.

PSYCHOLOGIST'S WRITTEN REPORTS

Psychologists are continually writing reports of various kinds. They write professional reports to each other and to professional administrative superiors and subordinates. Reports are prepared for the courts, juvenile authorities, labor unions, parents, and educational administrators, as well as for physicians, lawyers, and business executives. For the reader interested in the general topic of professional report writing, Huber (1961) has written a book covering many essentials for psychologists and psychiatrists. Super and Crites (1962) also devote a chapter to the topic. The report writing which concerns us, however, is for purposes of communication with our clients at a vocabulary level appropriate to their communication resources.

Without question, psychologists have been wise to follow the tested experience of physicians in many of their dealings with patients. However, it is unusual for a physician to write a report to his patients at the end of a course of treatment. Oral report is a common practice. It is equally unusual for a psychotherapist to write a report to a patient under the same set of conditions. But when dealing with *clients* at a cognitive level, in a complex process which requires extensive client learning, and which may involve marked behavior changes in some instances, communication supplemental to the interview is indicated as a most desirable practice.

On previous pages bibliocommunication has been considered at some length. Attention has been drawn to the need for information and concepts which need study as well as discussion. It is doubtful that clients, even when full attention has been devoted to clarification of relationship and process, will reach the end of the process of psychoevaluation with a clear understanding and memory of all important stages along the way. The purpose of this section is to indicate the desirability of using a written report, or "monograph," on the psychologist-perceived salient points of the client and his journey.

All professional reports are difficult to write, but I have found that the personalized report to a client, *with* whom one has been studying, is one of the most difficult. If one is writing an assessment report, the dimensions are quite definite, the criteria for assessment can be clearly stated, and comparisons with reference groups are not too difficult to couch in appropriate terms. Statements can be qualified with "probable," "possible," "usually," "alternatives worth your consideration are," and a host of other somewhat meaningful clichés.

In the psychoevaluation report one tends to review the objectives of the process, the methods and the content, and the relationship of steps toward meeting these objectives. There is need to emphasize structures related to personality dimensions, learning, and personal and environmental statics and relative statics. Because the psychologist is not assessing or diagnosing in the manner of counseling or psychotherapy, he must write in terms of his perceptions of the client's self-understandings and images as revealed by the varied forms of communication. This is not reflection as the term is commonly used in psychotherapy, but rather a form of restatement and review in a systematic manner.

One will find some elements of assessment in the process. When this is so, and the data are relevant to client planning, the report will reflect assessment at the appropriate places. The report will frequently call for review of client-considered alternative plans, but these reviews seldom should contain value weights as to their order or excellence in the psychologist's opinion. The first person may be the most suitable form of address although this is not always the case.

The written report to the client is not the final step in psychoevaluation. It is preparation for the final interview or interviews. It is the last of the "homework assignments." If the closing interviews do not bring about consideration of important new aspects of the relationship, the report is the client's record of his experience as the psychologist interprets it.

One must keep in mind the ethical considerations of such a procedure. There is no intention that it be used as psychological consultation by mail. The protection on this point is its clear purpose to be used as content for terminal discussion. One must also know what kinds of material may cause difficulties with a litigious client. Even though private practitioners insure themselves, care must be exercised. If the process becomes psychotherapy en route, instead of psychoevaluation, or a combination of psychoevaluation, assessment, and communication, the desirability and the form of any report must be viewed in a different light. However, a mature, self-actualizing, normal individual, operating at a high cognitive level, has very close to a right to an excellent professional report.

SUMMARY OF COMMUNICATION

Communication has become increasingly recognized in the past decade as the heart of social interaction. Whether it be verbal or nonverbal, and it is both, humans do not work together or war upon each other without use of communication—unworthy when it is by our opponents; clear, concise, and faultlessly logical when our own. We have considered communication as a method for helping the normal individual to study himself. A major emphasis has been placed on client problems of adaptation and distribution, social and self.

The specific categories to which we have attended are the interview with limited objectives, records, personal documents, nonverbal communication, bibliocommunication, and the psychologist's written reports. Each of these has been discussed in a general manner and geared to Pepinsky's categories of conditions. Because adjustment (psychotherapy) problems are considered by many to arise and be treated through theory and methods not the same as those applicable to the normal individual, they have been passed by in this material with casual mention. The need for much greater research efforts in this field has been stressed.

Chapter 8

PSYCHOLOGISTS

THE PSYCHOLOGIST is an ubiquitous fellow. He is amazingly versatile, and his multipotentiality is startling. *The* psychologist, of course, exists only in his personal percepts and the divisional affiliations of the American Psychological Association. There are so many interesting applications of method and so many theories. Our exploratory drives have led us far too frequently to study the other fellow so that we have, at times, neglected the study of our own professional problems. Our purpose here is to consider the professional psychologist and attempt to see him in relationship to a rapidly changing scene—the dynamics of the psychologist and of his culture and subcultures. In order to avoid the choppy and continual references to relevant items in the literature, the practice in some other parts of the book is deserted and a bibliography is provided at the end of the chapter.

In terms of the psychologist's work, some rather dusty back roads will be traversed. The reader may have noticed the sparse references to the emotion-encrusted and eroded labels, *clinical, counseling, industrial,* and *vocational.* This is intentional. Too many fruitless battles have been fought under these banners. The desires of groups so labeled to be *the* psychologist, while very human and understandable, has hindered us in many ways in our attempts to be self-actualizing as individuals and groups.

Some clarification and lessening of disagreement may be possible by considering the psychologist in professional practice in terms of his major functions, or areas, of service. Broad categories which describe psychological effort are *research, teaching,* and *professional service.* Although these categories are interdependent, the expected status hierarchies apply to them and, as one would expect, to the subdivisions within each. Research appears to be at the top, with physiological research the most respectable. Teaching, which usually demands some bows to research, comes in second place. Professional practice rates lowest, but within this category, clinical practice has the most status and counseling the least. Said in another way, those who are professionally closest to a medical practice with patients enjoy some of the physicians' reflected popular regard, while those who deal with the normal are less well known and less visible. None of these statements is particularly surprising. One would expect this ordering.

However, as was indicated in Chapter 1, it is possible to shift the stereotyped loadings if we consider what kinds of problems the professional psychologist attends to. In order to do this it appears desirable to define terms again. Rather than invent new words, or seriously distort or erode present ones, we turn again to English and English (1958). The first word is *adaptation:*

adaptation: *n.* **1.** originally change in structure or behavior that has survival value; now, more generally, any beneficial change to meet environmental demand. **2.** settling down to the conditions for work or learning, with the elimination of unnecessary preparatory behavior.

In addition to the dictionary definition above, a sharpening of the meaning of *adaptation* to avoid its use as a synonym for *adjustment* is provided by Cattell (1950, 261–262):

The term *adaptation* is best retained in the basic biological and social sense. The individual organism is well adapted to its environment when its behavior assures normal chances of survival to itself and to the society of which its offspring are part. To be realistic this must include adaptations to moral as well as physical facts; for a society of amoral people does not survive and a gangster may be shot by the police. Adaptation to morals is part of survival. It may then be objected that to examine the success of an individual's adaptation involves going beyond psychology, and indeed it does if our psychology is one which ignores society, morals, and biological survival. The fact that psychology is not competent to pass judgment on moral values or problems of biological survival, however, does not mean that it must ignore them, nor is it sufficient for psychologists to recommend a personality adjustment, however agreeable, which is not consistent with the survival of the individual or the species.

What we are attempting to establish here is that survival may not be only a matter of adjustment. As will be noted again later on, one can be exceedingly well adjusted and perish in that condition through lack of adaptation. I am reminded of the quick-frozen mammoth in Siberia, found with a full stomach and a buttercup dangling in his lips. The score in this example is Adjustment 100—Adaptation 0. Adaptation has lost much of its force in psychology as a matter of biological survival. In our culture the scalpel, hypodermic needle, antibiotics, and chemicals have become the instruments for biological survival. And they are not the implements of the psychologist. *Adaptation for psychological survival,* however, is very real, and the psychologist represents a highly skilled use of the tools of communication in that regard.

Some discussion is indicated by the use of the word survival coupled with psychological. The individual whose adaptation is so poor that he threatens his society not only by failure to make any valued contribution but also by becoming a subtraction item from societies' resources may be considered as an example of failure to survive psychologically. The situation is seen most clearly in terms of the man or woman who must be institutionalized permanently, or for long periods, because of lack of flexibility in meeting externalized problems (adaptation) or inability to maintain an appropriate internalized equilibrium (adjustment). A more detailed discussion has been encountered in the chapter devoted to personality and so we need not labor here.

The psychologist working with the normal individual who is having difficulty with problems of adaptation needs information, assurance, and skills in directions significantly different from those of the psychologist who is more concerned with problems of adjustment. We cannot ignore the efficiency variables of aptitude, ability, and achievement. One obvious difference is emphasis on the statics and dynamics of the culture and subcultures with which the individual must cope—the second dynamic. A second difference is the relative emphasis on the nomothetically based skills of assessment. A third and major difference has to do with the psychologist himself and his pattern of personality dimensions, which determines to some heavily weighted but unknown extent the fact that he does have greater facility for, and more personal satisfaction from, working with problems of adaptive behavior than with those of adjustment (psychotherapy).

Our second word of importance is *adjustment.* Again our beginning is with English and English:

adjustment: n. **1.** a static equilibrium between an organism and its surroundings in which there is no stimulus evoking a response, no need is unsatisfied, and all the continuative functions of the organism are proceeding normally. Such complete adjustment is never attained; it is a theoretical end of a continuum of degrees of partial adjustment. **2.** a condition of harmonious relation to the environment wherein one is able to obtain satisfaction for most of one's needs and to meet fairly well the demands, physical and social, put upon one. RELATIVE ADJUSTMENT (the only actual kind). **3.** the process of making the changes needed, in oneself or in one's environment, to attain relative adjustment.

To maintain parallel structure we again use Cattell (1950, 263–264) to sharpen the term for its use in these pages:

In popular psychology this much-used term means anything from the passive toleration of the morally intolerable to the earning of a large income! To gain a concept that means something, let us begin by paring away the meanings that belong to other concepts. In the first place, it is possible for a person to be adjusted but not adapted. For example, a man may be free from conflicts or repressions so long as he expresses himself criminally, or takes opium, or maintains some dangerous, exciting hobby, none of which is compatible with survival. Or a well-to-do, voluntarily childless woman may be perfectly happy with the "sublimations" of social distraction into which her maternal interests have disappeared. But she is not adapted, for a society whose women are wholly of this type would perish.

Similarly, as we have seen, it is possible for a man to be adapted but not adjusted, as seen in many severe neurotics who nevertheless hold jobs. However, in this case the loss of energy by internal friction always to some extent detracts from the final soundness of the adaptation. Indeed, *in general,* adaptation and adjustment will tend to go together. If for example, one has contemplated psychological adjustments and adaptations in relation to the recent war, he sees that the soldier who dies for his country in the complete faith of courage is both adapted and adjusted, whereas the neurotic is neither, for his internal adjustment is miserable and his external adaptation is not such as would permit his group to survive.

Obviously, in these two concepts, there are no sharp divisions which permit clear dichotomies. At times one will consider either as cause or effect or both. On the one hand, the emphasis is on personal and group survival, biological or psychological; on the other, tension, or drive reduction control conditions much more loaded with considerations which are internalized and related to the feelings of well-being of the individual. Serious maladaptation or maladjustment, or combinations of the two, can destroy the individual psychologically and harm his society. Problems are evident concerning whether *the* psychologist or the psychologist can, or should, deal adequately with all clients and patients. There are also problems of educating and training individuals who plan to enter professional psychology. These matters will be given space later in the chapter. We turn now to a third word, *distribution.*

English and English (1958) do not define the term in the sense that it is used here. Super (1957), Roe (1956), Darley and

Hagenah (1955), Cottle and Downie (1960), Wolfle (1954), Super and Crites (1962), and many others have assigned major space to the processes of the social and self-distribution of the individual. Our educational system, from the first grade through graduate school; business and industry; the government; and the military—all make heavy investments of staff, time, and money in order to improve the assignment of individuals to places in their work, educational and career hierarchies. From a deterministic standpoint, something is done to us for purposes of group survival. It seems reasonable to consider this aspect of distribution as a subcategory under adaptation. However, we also distribute ourselves. This *self-distribution* has varying application in our formal education, social activities, choices of occupations, selection of our homes, and numerous other facets of social living. Self-distribution appears also to be attached strongly to adaptation, but in the latter the adjustment dimensions seem to be more important than in the process of being distributed.

The professional psychologist has played a major role in distribution. In our schools, the educational psychologist often is a specialist in the selection and distribution of pupils and students. In the world of work, the personnel departments use psychologically derived methodologies and psychologists. Even in our graduate schools, there are decisions—college, department, and faculty-member made—which determine acceptance or rejection in the major and minor fields of concentration and whether or not the candidate achieves his diploma-certified goals.

THE FUNCTIONS OF ADAPTATION, ADJUSTMENT, AND DISTRIBUTION AS DESCRIPTION OF THE PROFESSIONAL PSYCHOLOGIST'S WORK

On the first page of this chapter the conviction was expressed that we had eroded the meaning of clinical, counseling, industrial, and vocational to an extent that makes them somewhat useless as descriptions of what psychologists bearing these labels do. The problem is somewhat confounded by the embedding of the terms in the divisional structure of the American Psychological Association. Because the 1960 decade gives indications that the structure of professional psychology, with particular reference to graduate education, is undergoing rapid reappraisal, this section of the chapter has some elements of prophesy.

Clinical Psychology

English and English (1958) define clinical psychology as:

> . . . that branch of psychology which deals with the psychological knowledge and practice employed in helping a client who has some behavior or mental disorder to find better adjustment and self-expression. It includes training and actual practice in diagnosis, treatment, and prevention, as well as research for the expansion of knowledge.—*Distg. fr.* psychiatry, which is a medical specialty.

Although clinical psychology, like the other psychologies being considered, is almost anything a writer or speaker wishes it to mean, it seems reasonable to stay with the relatively standard definition above. One of the problems of the term is that those who call themselves clinical psychologists hold state certificates for practice as such, are ABEPP diplomates in the specialty, identify with the definition words *diagnosis* and *treatment,* but do not represent a particularly homogeneous group either in training or in practice.

There has been a steady increase in the number of psychologists, usually designated as clinical, who have become staff members in hospitals and medical schools. Although practices differ widely from situation to situation, and person to person, many of these psychologists tend to refer to themselves as *medical psychologists.* In some medical schools the academic rank is *professor of psychiatry,* not only of psychology. There is also a strong tendency for those whose professional training has emphasized the illnesses usually labeled psychoneuroses, psychoses, psychosomatic or mental, to at times spread practice into the more nomothetic areas of adaptation and distribution. The range of practice in all of the psychological specialties is wide, sometimes appearing to have little relationship to previous training or experience.

Perhaps clinical psychology can be more sharply seen in terms of the personality theories most frequently found in training institutions, the use of diagnostic methodologies characterized, for example, by projective devices and very heavy reliance on the interview as treatment and communication. There is, of course, no territorial limit for psychological specialties as clear as there appears to be between constitutional and criminal law, or neurosurgery and pediatrics. It may be that if we combine a pattern of practice emphasis, based upon appropriate graduate and post-graduate training, such as ADJUSTMENT-Adaptation-distribution we have contributed a bit more toward clarity of practice understanding for the adjustment psychologist.

Counseling Psychology

Counseling psychology has had its difficulties in seeking identity. *Counseling* has become, for many, as generic (and meaningless) as guidance. Even in our authority, English and English, the confusion is great as one tries to find a central meaning. The dictionary does describe *counseling psychologist* as:

> . . . a professional psychologist who specializes in counseling. His training equips him to deal with personal problems not classified as mental illness, though they may be sequels or corollaries of mental or physical illness, e.g., the academic, social, or vocational problems of students.

From the definition one may conclude that there are two distinguishing marks: (1) the client of the counseling psychologist is the normal individual, and (2) practice is largely focused on formal education and with students. There is the further implication that this psychologist tends to limit his practice to the life career age group of *becoming*—clients falling, for the most part, in the age range from fifteen to thirty.

As is true in all labeled psychological specialties, those who identify with this designation practice over a wide range of professional psychology. But the modal employment distribution is in education with primary attention to problems of adaptation and distribution. Although there appears to be consensus among counseling psychologists that individual *assessment* is their major data collecting and interpreting process, neither Warren nor English and English define the word. Even in the book, *Assessment of men* (1948) the process is described but not defined. Everyone uses the word and knows what it means, but definition is difficult to find in a psychological source. It is used here to indicate "the matching, measuring, or comparing, of specified human personality dimensions against criteria deemed valid for predicting designated (relatively narrow) future behavior." *Evaluate* is given a more global meaning and has the feeling tone of "appreciation," both by Warren and English and English.

If we apply the three-functional-criteria pattern to the counseling psychologist, the most logical patterns seem to be ADAPTATION-Adjustment-distribution, or DISTRIBUTION-Adaptation-adjustment. It should be noted that these judgments place the counseling psychologist closer than the psychotherapist to those working in business and industry.

Industrial Psychology

If clinical psychology is defined by *behavior* or *mental disorders* and *diagnosis* and *treatment* and counseling psychology by its work setting and the age range of its clients, then industrial psychology might be said to be defined by the source of its practitioners' incomes. English and English say:

> . . . the scientific investigation of industrial problems by the methods, concepts, and principles of psychology and utilization of the findings to increase efficiency. Industry is here used in a very comprehensive sense, to include both business and the executive activities of government. The range of activity of *industrial psychology* is equally great: *personnel* selection and training, employee *morale, human engineering,* psychology of advertising and salesmanship, consumer need surveys, etc.—*Cp.* ECONOMIC PSYCHOLOGY the study of the working of the economic system as a whole, which utilizes the findings of industrial psychology in that wider context.

It is not unfair to rephrase the definition to mean that any psychologist who receives payment for psychological services to industry (in the comprehensive sense) is an industrial psychologist. Every known label for psychologists has undoubtedly found itself within the industrial fold. Although this statement indicates that every one of our service functions, adaptation-adjustment-distribution, has played the leading role in industrial situations, much of industrial practice is geared to the word "efficiency" in the definition. The patterns of practice tend, therefore, to be somewhat similar to, or identical with, those of many counseling or vocational psychologists—DISTRIBUTION-Adaptation-adjustment, or, ADAPTATION-Distribution-adjustment. There are, of course, many examples where ADJUSTMENT is the lead word.

Vocational Psychology

Counseling psychology, we said earlier, "has had its difficulties in seeking identity." Of vocational psychology one might remark that "it is an identity seeking a psychology." English and English have seven entries beginning with vocational, but no "vocational psychology." Clark (1957, 139) indicates the importance of vocational psychology by including it as one of twelve major categories of psychology. Of the problem he says:

> In the first place, it was difficult to determine where to put vocational psychologists. Some of these persons might well be classified with educational and developmental psychologists. Others, however, ought to be classified with industrial psychologists.

For whatever reasons, the vocational psychologist, although his contributions are important and numerous, does not have a professional homeland in the divisional structure of the American Psychological Association. The importance of an occupation is stressed in psychology, especially in its status and value aspects for the male in our culture. Many of the great figures in psychology have contributed consistently or intermittently to its research and application.

Perhaps one of the difficulties is the changed and changing position of the National Vocational Guidance Association. This organization in the 1920, and part of the 1930, decade was a professional home for most of the psychologists, and nonpsychologists, with a major interest in the vocational aspects of living. As the American Psychological Association increased its memberships in the professional areas, the NVGA more and more became a threshold professional organization heavily loaded with nonpsychologists. The result appears to be that the vocational psychologists divided themselves among the federated divisions in the APA and, while continuing to contribute heavily in many directions, did not establish a home with an identifying label.

In our three categories many primarily vocational psychologists appear to match with the ADAPTATION-Distribution-adjustment, or DISTRIBUTION-Adaptation-adjustment practitioners. Sociologists have shown increasing interest in the cultural dimensions of vocations and have tended to provide increasing and important research and practice in areas formerly of major interest to vocational psychologists.

Psychologists Not in Professional Practice

The American Psychological Association has reflected the frictions to be found in the psychology departments of colleges and universities in the attempts to strike a balance between the groups of psychologists who are chiefly interested in, and devote most of their time to, theory, teaching, and research and those who apply psychology as a profession. The two groups are, of course, interdependent, and either one would have great difficulty surviving without the other. Professional psychologists depend on the theorist and the researcher for much of the content of their practice. At budget time, particularly in the large publicly supported universities, community service and the application of theory to practical problems are not without their influence in obtaining funds for laboratories, research assistants, and clerical help. To emphasize these points we quote Clark (1957, 18–19):

These data support the earlier generalizations, and in fact suggest that persons whose interests resemble those of the founders of the APA (Developmental, Experimental and Physiological, General, Personality, Quantitative and Social) are now outnumbered two-to-one by persons whose interests are in more recently developed applications of psychology (Clinical, Counseling, Educational, School, Human Engineering, Industrial and Personnel).

Shift in interests can be revealed in another way also; in terms of the place of employment of psychologists. The academic setting no longer accounts for almost all members. The use of psychologists in both the military and civilian branches of the government in all kinds of capacities ranging in nature from administrative to technical demonstrates a significant change in the public perception of the status of psychology, as does the presence of psychologists in industries, schools, social agencies, hospitals, and in private practice.

The writer is inclined to view the points of difference among and between the "pure" and professional groups in psychology as evidences of cultural dynamics. Where social needs seem to exist and there is public support to meet these needs, someone will meet them. Formal education and social welfare agencies are particularly sensitive to the demands of the public. Although the methodologies originated, developed, or sharpened by psychology bear its label and stamp, other professional groups are flatteringly willing to make use of them. School counselors who practice psychology tend to be trained in schools of education. Psychotherapists with degrees and certificates in social welfare are not usually trained in departments of psychology. Personnel workers in business and industry frequently have degrees from schools of business administration. Many schools of engineering have curricula which are, or can be, labeled psychology.

Within psychology there are vexing problems which separate the two groups. One is the nature and purpose of the Ph.D. degree. Another is whether or not professional status should be gained with the granting of the Ph.D. degree or deferred as a post-graduate experience. There is turmoil as the "angel" of professional psychology, the Veterans Administration, alters its policies in keeping with the changes in the hospital populations. On the one hand, the older more institutionalized patients do not afford the breadth of practice students would like; on the other, the Veterans Administration does not appear to be completely happy with some of the graduate trainees in psychology who are being sent to them by the universities.

There is some reason to believe that what has been said above is important to the self-actualization of psychologists whose goals are professional, rather than research and academic. If psychologists in embryo are strongly attracted to "diagnosis-patient," they will do well to consider medical psychology and a willingness to work in medical settings, conforming to the legitimate medical control under which their work must be done. Medicine has been hardheaded, but quite reasonable, in accepting the contributions of psychology. There is little evidence that hospitals or medical schools will relinquish control to departments of psychology or to individual psychologists. Hathaway (1958) is good required reading for any psychologist who chooses the diagnosis-*patient* route.

If there is strong attraction to "assessment-*client*," the young psychologist has other routes to travel. Personality theory, learning theory, social and developmental psychology all make approaches, theoretical and instrumental, which are concentrated on the hero of this book—*the normal individual.* And hanging over one's head is also the specter of mathematics and statistics and two-way communication with digital and analog computers. The choices of our psychologist in training may be more easily made, with higher validity and reliability, if the semantic ghosts of the past and their emotionally conditioned champions can be buried by more pointed, less eroded terms.

THE PRACTITIONER'S "TO," "FOR," AND "WITH" PROBLEMS

Consideration has been given above to the dimensions of research-teaching professional practice and to adaptation-adjustment-distribution functions in professional practice. Attention is directed now to the conditions of psychologist-client control—*to, for,* and *with* clients. These conditions appear to be of importance when we take into account what it is we attempt to do in our client relationships. If we consider these words as descriptions of the amount of psychologist control of relationship, we can present them as in Figure 5.

Figure 5 Psychologist Control of Client Relationship: TO-FOR-WITH

TO, strong-to-complete psychologist control	*FOR, shifting psychologist-client control*	*WITH, strong-to-complete client control*
Patients, candidates for employment or promotion, admission to educational opportunities, children	*Rehabilitation, counseling psychology, mild psychotherapy, information-giving, and advice*	*Psychoevaluation, listening therapy*

As appears true of adaptation-adjustment-distribution, it is almost impossible to find situations which are completely *to, for,* or *with.* When a medical psychologist aids in, or is completely responsible for, diagnosis, he is doing something *to* the patient. He would also insist that he is doing something *for* him. *With,* in our sense, is for most practical purposes absent. When a candidate for employment, or promotion, subjects himself to the psychologist's methodologies, the psychologist is doing something *to,* will insist that he is also doing something *for,* and under some circumstances will believe, rightfully, that he is working *with* the individual. However, the loading of psychologist control in these situations is so clear that we can place them toward the *to* end of the continuum.

It seems that, with few exceptions, when we diagnose, assess, evaluate, or impose a quite rigid structure of psychologist-client relationship, we are loading the *to* to a greater extent than the *for* or *with.* Because planned lack of structure is a form of structure, the most avowedly "permissive" psychologist does things to his clients. Many psychologists dislike the word *to* in this setting, as it is of the same nature as *manipulation* and *prescription.* However, one need not (should not?) attach value weights to the terms. We do describe psychotherapy as "the manipulation of client anxiety levels." Also without question, we do *prescribe.* If one diagnoses or assesses, he will often describe (prescribe) orally what the client and patient can, and should, do in order to relieve tensions; sublimate; move toward, away from, or at, elements in the environment; and gain necessary information, assurance, or skill. We have been most reluctant to permit our obvious prescriptions to appear with that label in the literature. For one thing, this would expose us to outcome research, a most abhorrent condition. For another, however much we follow our prescriptions with individual clients, our lacks of assurance (modesty?) and need for favorable feedback (avoidance of criticism?) seem to inhibit us from removing our masks of practice so neatly held in place by our professional roles. Much of the problem is related to our being "talking," not "working" doctors. It is most difficult to give definitive prescriptions for doing things to, for, or with people if one relies on a single methodology—the interview—however flexible it appears. Perhaps part of this dilemma will be solved when we consider communication more broadly (see Chapter 7).

The *for* relationships appear to be present always. It is difficult to imagine a psychologist in professional practice who would not insist that he did things *for* his patients and clients. Client perception of the *for* can be expected to be, at times, different from that of the psychologist. Counseling psychology has tended to emphasize the *for* and the *with,* while the traditional clinical psychologist has tended to emphasize the *with.* If the client retains control of the alternatives to be selected and followed, we have moved away from the *to* and are moving through the *for* with an increasing loading of *with.*

A "pure" *with* relationship, with the client in complete control throughout the span of the relationship, is perhaps an impossibility. Nor is permissiveness a synonym for with. However, in situations where the psychologist plays the role of the listener only, we have many of the elements. In psychoevaluation, where an individual is studying himself, the *with* is predominant but the *for* and *to* are both there to at least a limited extent. The need for structure or "structured lack of structure" foils our attempts at purity. We also encounter in Pepinsky's (1948) categories of lack of information, lack of skill, lack of assurance, and choice-anxiety conditions which indicate that the client cannot take complete charge until certain minimal learnings take place.

It is evident that our continuum of client-psychologist relationship control is governed in large part by situational perceptions. Acceptance to student status in a law school is a process which demands that the social rites of passage to be a lawyer take precedence over the individual's desires, needs, and wants. We do something to him and for him. The paraplegic with work skills that require only that we find, or help to find, a job is one *for* whom something may be done. The self-actualizing, normal, mature individual who wishes to study himself and his future in a cultural setting much more strongly enters the *with* relationship. There are no good or bad connotations to any of the terms we have used when the processes have survival values for individuals or groups, biologically, socially, or psychologically. There are times when we legitimately and ethically diagnose, assess, and evaluate; teach, research, and practice professionally; deal with problems primarily adaptive, adjustive, or distributive; and do things to, for, and with people. Our only strong reservation is that we have yet to meet the psychologist who has all, or most, of these skills to an extent which gives high-level performance in all situations with all clients. The analogy to the physician who claims to be an exceedingly competent psychiatrist, surgeon, neurosurgeon, pediatrician, opthalmologist, radiologist, internist, and hospital administrator, all at the same time, is not too farfetched.

PERSONALITY DIMENSIONS AND WHAT PSYCHOLOGISTS DO

As one reads the references applying to the foregoing and following materials in this chapter, he will discover that not much attention has been given to the evidence regarding why one psychologist becomes a psychotherapist and another, using some of the same basal psychological material, becomes a distributor of people. In truth, psychology in general has not researched the selection and training of its own graduate candidates with nearly the rigor and effort it has applied to distribution problems in the fields of others.

There have been intriguing hints over the past twenty years that personality dimensions and patterns play a major part in determining the directions which psychologists take within the field. Kreidt (1949, 1952) presents data involving the measured interests of various kinds of psychologists. Trends are demonstrated which seem worthy of more intensive examination. Kelly and Fiske (1950) discovered that interest measurement with the Strong Vocational Interest Blank did have a significant bearing on the success of budding psychotherapists in the Veterans Administration training program. Strong (1951) and Strong and Tucker (1952) demonstrated the permanence of the patterns measured by the blank and their effectiveness in the selection of a medical specialty. Adkins (1954) did a factor analysis pertaining to the divisional structure of the APA. The results indicated that differences existed among and between the groups.

Roe (1956), although her approaches were necessarily idiographic, arrived at conclusions that indicate support for hypotheses pertinent to personality differences as indicators of vocational directions. Darley and Hagenah (1955) consider measured interest patterns in this light and also formulate their theory of the *professional trap* as an explanation of related phenomena. Certainly Super (1957) and Super and Crites (1962) did not miss the implications of much of the research above as well as the data accumulating in Super's ongoing study of career development.

Related to the work which has been reported in regard to the Strong Vocational Interest Blank and frequently appearing in the same sources is that reported in regard to the Allport-Vernon-Lindzey Scale of Values. Darley and Hagenah (1955) comment on the relationships between this instrument and the Strong blank. Cattell (1957) presents a mass of material drawn from his L, Q, and T data, which bear on the problems of personality dimensions and patterns and their relationships to career activities.

Use of the Miller Analogies Test for graduate students has also contributed information about distribution problems. The manual for the test gives quite clear evidence that, whatever it is measuring, there are substantial relationships between scores and success in pursuit of the Ph.D. degree in many graduate schools. In some major university departments of psychology, the award of the doctorate is indeed rare for those whose raw score is below 65. The test seems to predict well for course content quantitative in nature, although in the original Form G, only one-fourth of the items were considered as based on a Q factor.

Although the author has been collecting Miller analogies scores, Strong blank results, and the Allport-Vernon-Lindzey scale patterns of his graduate students for over fifteen years, no thoroughgoing analysis of the data has been made. Some of the data appear to support hypotheses indicated above. The interest patterns of those who have followed careers related to problems of adaptation and distribution appear to differ from those who have become primarily interested professionally in problems of adjustment. Those of us who are "rockheads" will deal with adaptation and distribution; our esteemed "bleeding-heart" colleagues will continue to attend primarily to better patient adjustment.

TRAINING PROGRAMS

For almost two decades the Veterans Administration has provided financial support for professional psychology training programs in colleges and universities. Immediately following World War II, this support was directed to providing services for the veteran in order that he might adapt, distribute himself, and be distributed to civilian life. From this program, under the original direction of Dr. Ira Scott, many of the present college and university psychological service and counseling centers developed. As the wave of veterans for whom these services were appropriate subsided, the hospital programs centering on problems of adjustment developed. The need for primary emphasis on adaptation and distribution weakened, except for the brief bulge stemming from the Korean War.

In terms of graduate training in professional psychology, the adjustment emphasis has been a boon to those who wished to be psychotherapists. However, this has not been an unmixed blessing because, unlike the immediate post war programs, universities and colleges have not followed through in providing campus internships and practice in the same manner that characterized the provision of professional psychological services from 1945 to 1950. Unless, for example, psychology departments turn their training efforts much more strongly to practicum and internship problems of the aging, as well as to the normal and mentally ill, a serious vacuum will develop. Where do, and will, our graduate trainees turn for supervised experience when the Veterans Administration no longer can follow the programs of the past several years? It is true that medical schools will provide excellent training facilities for medical psychologists and ancillary psychological skills as they have done in the past. However, this is an answer for a minority of the graduate-level trainees. Turning young psychologists loose to "observe" in low-level programs of various kinds will not satisfy them, or many of us. Unpaid assignments will inflict undesirable effects both on selection and the final product.

Possible Directions

If we assume that adequate supervised experience in professional psychology is a function of the university, through the psychology department, we should seek answers on the campus as well as in the community. Because this book is concerned with the problems of the normal, with emphasis on adaptation and distribution, we need not concern ourselves deeply with serious adjustment problems such as must psychotherapy and its training programs. Nor does it seem reasonable that universities under present conditions will be able in general to provide completely the minimal adequate budgets for our purpose.

The suggestion here is consideration of a federated program of psychological services on the campus. Although not all the services used as examples below will be found universally on university campuses, the general pattern will be. The following are frequently provided.

For students:

Educational-vocational counseling
Reading and study-skill groups
Adjustment aids for the normal
Personal assessment
Social skill practica
Speech therapy and skills

For colleges, schools, and departments within the university:

Centralized machine scoring of classroom examinations
Administration and scoring of regional and national test programs
Admission and competence testing
Evaluation of individual cases

For the community:

Consultation services
Testing, scoring, and test result interpretation for business and industry and private educational programs
Personal assessment and evaluation for individuals
Cooperative and subsidized or contract research
Seminars, clinics, and adult education classes, for bringing professional workers up to date on advances in their fields

The above is not exhaustive, but examples of what is to be found are sufficient for our purpose. Although universities and private psychologists have offered many of these services to the community under varying circumstances, the author is not aware of any truly comprehensive program of combined student-community psychological services. In some situations there is hope that unified efforts by psychology departments, schools of education, schools and departments of social welfare, and departments of educational psychology will result in a comprehensive research-training-service effort. Certain goals appear of major importance.

1. *A cooperatively planned program.* Few psychology departments may be eager to undertake the managerial functions of such a project. Nor is this always necessary. The usual pattern is a number of independent or quasi-independent programs with overlapping of staff, physical facilities, and budget expenditures. Purchasing and equipment pooling can frequently lower overall university costs. Research can often be facilitated by the cooperation of staff and program members. Clerical costs and staff can sometimes be pooled.

2. *Geographically central and common physical facilities.* There is more than a grain of truth in the statement that we "see our campus colleagues only at national and regional conferences and conventions." Not only is a "one-stop filling station" more convenient, the attendants are likely to know each other. Trading of present scattered space for a central location is at times not only possible but advantageous to more than one program on a campus.

3. *More significant research programs.* This point is obvious. There are advantages and disadvantages to group research projects. Under some conditions this approach is the most productive. Geographical proximity and greater and better physical and budget resources should be an aid to research and research grants. There should be no need to interfere with the research efforts of the individual.

4. *Community services can provide for some of the costs of the program.* This common practice of making services available to the community on a fee basis needs no elaboration. In addition, there are circumstances under which students will receive more, and/or better, services for their fees under a more comprehensive approach.

5. *University control and supervision of internships and practica.* Excellent as many of our community resources for these purposes are, they are not numerous enough nor do they afford the breadth of experience we often believe essential for the training of professional psychologists and allied workers. Our guilt feelings might subside to some extent if we could assume more direct responsibility for what happens to our advisees.

A second approach is the centralized line structure, rather than the federated organization above. Which is preferred, or necessary, is a matter of local conditions. The centralized line program may have difficulties in terms of the status and autonomy of existing services and service personnel. It does have advantages relative to more unified action, closer budget control, and speed of decision.

The third approach includes the essential community resources for internships and practica of various kinds. Both the entirely campus program and the ones wholly dependent on the community have obvious weaknesses from the standpoint of training experiences for graduate students. The community provides a greater variety of conditions and cases than is usually possible on campus. It suffers as a complete training resource from its necessary service operations which must have priority over teaching and research. There are also difficulties in providing supervision which is so essential. Programs entirely on the campus do provide better supervision and control of the training elements, but they tend to have limited types of clients. Artificiality must be guarded against constantly.

In this chapter the effort has been made to analyze certain major groups of professional psychologists in regard to their names, work habits and places, APA habitat, and what their futures may hold. It seemed necessary that this be done in order to consider the psychologist best qualified to work *with* the normal, self-actualizing individual who has escaped from becoming and has not fallen yet into the clutches of gerontologists. Before turning to this psychologist in the following chapter, the reader is again informed that the chief bibliographical items, for this chapter, follow. As was stated in the beginning, citations were held to a minimum in the running text for purposes of better coherence.

SUGGESTED READINGS

Astin, A. W. 1961. The functional autonomy of psychotherapy. *Amer. Psychol.*, **16:** 75–77.

Ausubel, Cyril. 1961. Personality disorder is disease. *Amer. Psychol.*, **16:** 69–75.

Burt, Cyril. 1958. The inheritance of mental ability. *Amer. Psychol.*, **13:** 1–16.

Deutsch, Cynthia P. 1958. What price psychology? *Amer. Psychol.*, **13:** 645–652.

Division 5 Test Use Committee. 1958. Graduate training programs in evaluation and measurement. *Amer. Psychol.*, 13: 467–470.

Guilford, J. P. 1959. Three faces of intellect. *Amer. Psychol.*, **14:** 469–479.

Hahn, M. E. 1955. Counseling psychology. *Amer. Psychol.*, **10:** 279–282.

Hathaway, Starke R. 1958. A study of human behavior: the clinical psychologist. *Amer. Psychol.*, 13: 257–265.

Katzell, R. A., and Thompson, A. S. 1958. Some comments on "After Legislation." *Amer. Psychol.*, 13: 109–112.

Kelley, N. H., Sanford, F., and Clark, K. E. 1961. The meaning of the ABEPP diploma. *Amer. Psychol.*, **16:** 132–142.

Rogers, Carl. 1958. A process conception of psychotherapy. *Amer. Psychol.*, **13:** 142–150.

Rychlak, J. F. 1959. Clinical psychology and the nature of evidence. *Amer. Psychol.*, **14:** 642–648.

Rychlak, J. F. 1959. Clinical psychology and the nature of evidence. *Amer. Psychol.*, **14:** 633–637.

Smith, M. B. 1959. Research strategies toward a conception of positive mental health. *Amer. Psychol.*, **14:** 673–681.

Strong, E. K. 1958. Satisfaction and interests. *Amer. Psychol.*, **13:** 449–456.

Szasz, T. S. 1961. The uses of naming and the origin of the myth of mental illness. *Amer. Psychol.*, **16:** 59–66.

Van de Castle, R. L., and Eichhorn, O. J. 1961. Length of graduate training for experimental and clinical psychologists. *Amer. Psychol.*, **16:** 178–180.

White, R. W. 1958. When prophecy fails. *Amer. Psychol.*, **13:** 656–657.

Chapter 9

PSYCHOLOGISTS—THEIR KNOWLEDGES, SKILLS, AND PSYCHOEVALUATION

THIS FINAL chapter must be presented in terms of somewhat idealized images of the psychologist. The discussion is based on knowledges and insights which in all probability no single professional psychologist possesses. A society and culture based on youth worship does not always turn easily to face the realities forced on it by a steadily rising average citizen age. As has been indicated in the preceding chapter, few, if any, graduate schools are concentrating attention on a program which will produce new graduates qualified to step into the practice of psychoevaluation with the ink still moist on the diploma.

Even when there is faculty interest in this relatively quite small area of professional practice, no internships are known to the author which would provide essential supervised experiences under optimal conditions. The healthy, mature, normal, self-actualizing individual is not a major concern of hospitals. He, or she, is not usually found as a patient in Veterans Administration facilities. Relationships between private practitioners and departments of psychology are rarely of a nature which will encourage a large-scale internship program. In addition, unless one or two universities become regional or national centers for this psychological specialty, the costs for the small number of candidates may be prohibitive. But despite the difficulties there is a social need and demand, and psychologists and related disciplines are attempting to meet it as best they can.

What follows, then, is one man's view of desirable knowledges, experiences, and insights which would tend to make the psychologist better equipped to provide services to the group to which this book is devoted. The discussion will follow the headings *assessment, diagnosis, evaluation, psychoevaluation,* and *communication,* and the axes will include the *to, for,* and *with* relationships with clients. Major emphasis will be directed to problems of adaptation and distribution.

ASSESSMENT

In Chapter 1 a definitional description of the assessment process was provided. At that point it was indicated that *assessment involved a quite specific purpose;* i.e., job or career planning (usually short range); educational distribution to schools, colleges, or other formal training facilities; an aid to self-study; or a process to which the subject was forced to submit, such as an employment situation or assignment in the military. It was further implied that assessment is geared more closely to short-term prediction than is evaluation. Assessment was judged to be more closely identified with doing things to or for clients or subjects. Assessment was also considered as a process with greater application to the decades closer to becoming than to either the sowing or reaping periods of being. The older the self-actualizing individual is chronologically, the more we turn to evaluation and the less we depend on the kinds of assessment which are most useful at earlier ages. Assessment was also treated as the specialty of the professional counseling psychologist and to certain industrial psychologists. Mention is again made to representative materials regarding assessment which include Bingham (1937), Super (1949), Hahn and MacLean (1955), Cottle and Downie (1960), and Super and Crites (1962).

Although assessment as it is treated in these sources is not the level or kind of operation which appears appropriate for psychoevaluation, it is a *sine qua non* for much of evaluation and not of little importance for certain kinds of diagnosis. Perhaps its greatest importance from one standpoint is the emphasis on stressing the positive, socially useful and desirable personality attributes of the individual. There is light emphasis on therapy in the sense that something must be cured or radically changed (Hahn, 1955).

Assessment tends to be nomothetically based and has an actuarial cast. Psychometrics is its handmaiden. It seems probable that the greatest amount of professional psychological practice, in terms of number of clients and practitioners, is concerned primarily with assessment methodologies and theory. Its most direct importance in psychoevaluation is concerned with the distribution aspects of client self-planning. Assessment demands a solid grounding in the second dynamic. The specificity of client self-planning suits assessment techniques for personality matchings with many environmental dimensions. Thus it seems reasonable to expect the psychologist practicing psychoevaluation to have theoretical and professional competence in assessment.

If one can judge by employment opportunities for professional practitioners using assessment skills, the bulk of the openings can be filled by those with approximately two years of appropriate graduate training or the equivalent. The modal graduate degree seems to be the M.A. or M.S. in psychology and/or educational psychology. The minimal essentials include statistics covering central tendency, dispersion, tests of significance, correlation, and the standard principles and applications of variance and covariance. The first dynamic is not usually stressed at this level, although some familiarity with perception, motivation, and learning theory is usually included in the graduate curriculum. Because so many of the individuals working at the assessment level obtain their formal training in schools of education and departments of educational psychology, exposure to the second dynamic tends to be specifically related to the environment in formal educational institutions at the secondary school level—the second decade of becoming. Psychology departments which emphasize the M.A. or M.S. degrees offer the second dynamic in industrial settings rather than in formal educational situations. Institutions emphasizing the training program for subdoctoral-level school psychologists often combine psychotherapeutic emphases with those for the normal individual. Where training for rehabilitation counselors is provided at the two- or three-year graduate level, there is emphasis on both the medical and socioeconomic environment.

Much of the evidence indicates that assessment practice and graduate training is directed at the problems of distribution with varying loadings on adaptation and adjustment in broader settings. Personality and learning theory are not, indeed cannot be, deeply probed. There is not sufficient time. Communication is weighted at an information level with the interview carrying most of the load. The professional home of those who are primarily concerned with assessment tends to be the American Personnel and Guidance Association as much as in the American Psychological Association. The assessment psychologists may well carry the greatest client load of all.

Walter V. Bingham (1946) encapsulated much of assessment when he said:

> The question is: How intelligent is he (the soldier) now? What can he learn and how fast can he learn it? Neither is it a matter of practical concern to know what a soldier's *native* intelligence was at birth, before his mental development had been facilitated in any degree by stimulating surroundings or hampered by a stultifying environment. The assignment officer wants an index of what the new soldier can be expected to learn, rather than a figure which purports to tell what he might have been able to learn if he had had a better home, no enfeebling illness and a great deal more education.

DIAGNOSIS

Diagnosis is a word borrowed by psychologists from medical usage. English and English (1958) give as their first meaning, "identification of disease or abnormality from symptoms presented, and from a study of its origin and course." It implies a condition in which the individual diagnosed as being ill, or markedly deviate, cannot meet the adjustment problems present without professional help. Although adaptation and distribution factors are involved, they are seldom primary for psychotherapists. There is a strong weighting toward doing something to or for the person who has disturbing symptoms which indicate the probability of disease or abnormality. The word twin of *diagnosis* is *therapy*. A cure or an alleviation of a condition involving the first dynamic is a hoped-for outcome.

The adaptation-distribution psychologist rarely will have time in either his graduate training or practice to become also an adjustment psychologist. However, unless he is to harm some clients, he should know when to assess, when to evaluate, and when to diagnose. The diagnostic skills of nonpsychotherapists usually do, and should, reach a level of competence at which cases not within their clear professional capacity are referred to another more appropriate professional worker. The sword, of course, is two-edged. The adjustment psychologist should possess assessment and evaluative skills at a level which will prevent confusion of these processes with psychotherapy.

In current graduate training the psychologist qualified to diagnose will almost always have firm foundations in perception, personality and learning theory, motivation, and the physiological aspects of the central nervous system. In addition to these basic fields the first dynamic receives great attention. There is usually opportunity for reasonable exposure to ideographic orientations and to the penetration behind masks by use of interview techniques and various projective devices. Minimal skills in diagnosis are sharpened also if the internship involves some hospital exposure concentrated on carefully supervised professional relationships with the patients of medical and nonmedical psychotherapists. Although our adaptation-distribution psychologist may have no desire to be a therapist, there is no great excuse for his not developing diagnostic skills which will protect *his clients* and those who should be *the patients* of others.

Diagnosis takes the adjustment psychologist along training routes and into knowledges and skills which diverge rapidly from those of the psychologist whose major efforts are devoted to the normal individual. Because diagnosis tends to be concentrated on the covert, masked behaviors, recourse must be had in psychometrics to instruments quite different in nature from those used by the adaptation psychologist. Projective devices are much more often resorted to than the familiar aptitude, ability, and achievement tests. Clinical inference based on longitudinal case history data and interview content analysis is much in evidence. In many ways adjustment practice closely parallels that of medical practitioners, particularly the psychiatrist. To gain the minimal competencies both to assess and diagnose at a high level, even if we can safely ignore what appear to be radically different personality patterns in the professional practitioners of each, would add approximately two years to the graduate program. Diagnosis depends quite heavily on supervised practice with patients which introduces therapy as an almost unavoidable concomitant in training. This too lengthens the period of preparation for practice. With these, and other considerations in mind, it is not usual to find the psychologist who is a specialist in adaptation and distribution areas and who can also diagnose beyond a level necessary to avoid mistakenly having patients as clents.

EVALUATION

Evaluation is concerned with a more global analysis of an individual's personality dimensions interpreted in the situations, fields, and environment which have played major roles in shaping the unique person. Evaluation is long range and long-circuited. Usually we evaluate in terms of longer periods of time, past and future, than is true of assessment and, in many instances, diagnosis. Evaluation tends to be concerned with personality factors and environmental settings which are *predicted* in the assessment process. Put another way, we are concerned with what were the criteria for assessment or for short-range distribution purposes at an earlier age. Where, in assessment, we dealt with psychograms or psychometric profiles, in evaluation we turn to the more generalized and descriptive life patterns, life space, and life-styles.

In the projected companion volume to this one, attention will be given to the specific dimensions of personality for evaluation and assessment. Here we are concerned with the generalities. Because the psychologist must communicate with his clients in client language, the number and complexity of personality dimensions used in evaluation must conform, at least in part, to a least common semantic denominator. When we deal with the efficiency variables, categories must be more simplified than most of us like as psychologists. We utilize such rubrics as academic, clerical, mechanical, and artistic; things versus people; and practical versus theoretical. In the realm of other dimensions we may use, for example, conscience, self or self-images or concepts, reality testing, and the unconscious. Some will prefer such terms as ego or ego strength, super-ego, and id. When temperament is important, we utilize the simplest categories which retain meaning for both psychologist and client. If needs enter the picture, many of us turn to Maslow rather than Murray on the assumption that the law of parsimony may be better enforced.

The essence of evaluation is the assumption that, with the normal, mature individual, what he has been he will continue to be. We *assess* for job placement. We *diagnose* for illness or extreme deviation. We *evaluate* for careers and generalized future behavior. Assessment implies TO-For-with. Diagnosis also implies TO-For-with. Evaluation includes almost any loading of the to-for-with combinations depending on why evaluation is done. Assessment and diagnosis are frequently seen as processes in which the professional person has more situational control than the client or patient. Evaluation is usually seen as more situational control by the client. Our individual will continue to be what he has been, but he may operate more happily and efficiently if he has the information and insights which evaluation supplies to him. There are many situations in which evaluation is in a TO-For-with setting, but as has been stated above, this is less common than with assessment or diagnosis. Because there is often serious contamination of the WITH by the to-for in all three of the processes described above, *psycho-*

evaluation has been used as a term which means major loading with WITH.

Again we are faced with problems about where and how professional psychologists can obtain training. Strong financial support for the training of school counselors under the National Defense Education Act has increased markedly the opportunities for learning the fundamentals of assessment. The second dynamic in this program has been sharply focused on settings in formal education and on certain job and career preparation areas. The Veterans Administration has provided even greater support for the training of individuals who will concentrate on diagnosis and therapy in their professional careers. It was true that while certain sub-age groups still were present in the hospital populations, there were excellent supervised experiences for evaluation specialists. In rehabilitation programs also, there is a great need for evaluative procedures for a small but important proportion of the clients and patients. But psychologists with the Ph.D. degree, or its equivalent, have not turned in great numbers to service practice in rehabilitation.

A sticking point remains in evaluation for dealing with the second and third dynamics. We have done quite well with the more specific situations and environment such as hospital settings, formal educational institutions, and some phases of the military life. There appear to be few formalized offerings in graduate schools which prepare the graduate student for studying more generalized cultural and subcultural dynamics as settings within which people must live, adapt, adjust, distribute themselves, and be distributed. Nor is the material regarding the shifting goals and value systems of the normal individual in our culture, at various age periods and in differing socioeconomic settings, easily available to our practitioners in embryo. It would be unrealistic to urge that universities attempt the impossible and grant certificates of competence in an area such as this. But one can legitimately urge an ordering of our knowledge, theories, and hypotheses which will make self-education somewhat easier for the professional practitioner.

Excellent materials have been and are becoming available in the literature centered on the second and third dynamics. Examples are the handbooks from the University of Chicago Press: *Aging in Western Societies,* 1960, E. W. Burgess, Editor; *Handbook of Aging and the Individual,* 1959, J. E. Birren, Editor; *Handbook of Social Gerontology,* 1960, Clark Tibbetts, Editor. Industrial psychology curricula often include meaningful, but quite specific, materials concerned with special situations, fields, and environment. Developmental and social psychology courses are rich in pertinent data which, however, must be organized for use with individuals by the student. Our concentration on the dynamics of the individual personality with a much lesser emphasis on environment may be accurately reflected by the content and purpose of the journals published by the American Psychological Association. The first and third dynamics are quite well represented. The second dynamic has but one journal primarily devoted to it and this one is highly specific.

We take leave of evaluation at this point. In summary of the process it is again emphasized that evaluation rests heavily on a base of assessment skills. In the age period of *being* it is the method which appears most applicable of the three discussed above to the normal, mature, self-actualizing individual. A major concern of evaluation is with life pattern and life-style rather than assessment and crisis points. There has been less emphasis on evaluation in our graduate departments of psychology than on either diagnosis or assessment. This is understandable in the light of the professional experience necessary to move to a position of competence and assurance in dealing with older normal clients. Such people are not found in institutional settings with high frequency nor are they as available for intensive study as are patients. Internships which could promote this kind of competence more rapidly are indeed rare. Self-education and self-training may be the mode for some years to come.

PSYCHOEVALUATION

We return to the heart of the book. Psychoevaluation has been presented as a joint process involving a client who has sought a professional psychological service and a psychologist competent to provide it. An employer, family, governmental agency, or social organization could not "have John Jones psychoevaluated." These agents or agencies under some circumstances could have John Jones *assessed, diagnosed,* or *evaluated.* Under such circumstances something is done *to* or *for* John Jones, and *for* or *with* the third party. Only John Jones can be the agent when the client-psychologist *with* process is involved.

Psychoevaluation as has been stated is based on the skills of assessment, evaluation, and, to a lesser extent, diagnosis. If we consider some of the dimensions frequently encountered on previous pages as follows, perhaps the intended communication will be facilitated. Only the third column identifies a particular process.

		(Psychoevaluation)
diagnosis	*Assessment*	*EVALUATION*
to	*For*	*WITH*
adjustment	*Distribution*	*ADAPTATION*
therapy	*Counseling*	*COMMUNICATION*
	Becoming	*BEING and HAVING BEEN*

It is most difficult to identify any present graduate program in this country which can be said to be aiming at developing practitioners of the process of psychoevaluation. There are psychologists who so practice privately and in university public-service centers.

But the ones known to the writer have come from groups which carry such labels as counselors, consultants, or psychotherapists. They are, in the main, self-trained. They are also busy people. One apparently becomes a sound general psychologist, selects a departmentally approved professional specialty, and, in terms of individual personality dimensions and the vagaries of the second dynamic, moves into the specialization which in this book has been called psychoevaluation. There appears to be no present division in the American Psychological Association which provides a natural home for this small group of psychologists.

The last item of importance in reviewing our process is that of emphasis on the second and third dynamics. It has been the viewpoint in this book that the first dynamic is the special province of the psychotherapist. The second dynamic has been presented as "belonging" to the counselors of numerous specializations—the industrial psychologist, the social psychologist, and the vocational and educational psychologists. The third dynamic is the common property of all professional psychologists, but the tendency to specialize in the first or second often makes valid evaluation of interaction difficult. If $3 = 1 + 2$, when either 1 or 2 is missing 3 is also missing. If interaction of the first and second comprise the third, then there must be balance in understanding and in interpreting the first two. Of those practicing psychoevaluation, among other specialties, a self-imposed gain in knowledge of the dynamic weakest in graduate training and subsequent practice is essential.

Should a training need of any great proportions arise, the current small discussion groups of professional practitioners may well be formalized in terms of clinic-seminars provided by universities at the post-doctoral level. This pattern is a familiar one for specialties in any professional field. In terms of predoctoral offerings there is the possibility of better balance between the personality dynamics of the individual and those of the cultures and subcultures of which the individual is a part.

COMMUNICATION

Chapter 7 was devoted to this topic, and the detailed discussion of the elements of client-psychologist communication may be reviewed there. Here the intent is to reemphasize and highlight points considered earlier. Nonmedical psychotherapists followed many of the practices of the psychiatrist in dealing with the problems of personal adjustment. One of these shared practices is the tendency to use the interview as the chief, or only, avenue of patient-therapist communication. The counseling psychologist has made some use of bibliocommunication, structured and unstructured autobiographies, and the written psychologist's report to the client as a basis for the final interview, or interviews. However, these psychologists have tended to follow the lead of the psychiatrist and the adjustment psychologist in placing the major burden of communication on the interview. There is no intention of reviewing the inadequacies of the interview in certain professional relationships. For dealing with the mature, normal, self-actualizing individual at the cognitive level, the published reliabilities and validities in outcome research are far too low to rely greatly upon it to accomplish the hoped-for objectives.

If the major liability of the client is lack of critical information, there is a possibility that printed material may be far better for supplying the lack than a lecture or a discussion by the psychologist. If lack of skills is perceived by the client as a roadblock, it is possible that there are more efficient methods of building assets than just talking about the matter. Lack of assurance may well require more client-psychologist discussion, but lack of assurance may have as a base lack of information or lack of skills. Choice-anxiety partakes of some of the same rationale.

The research regarding personal documents as methods of individual evaluation has not yielded results which are particularly heartening, but those who have used the life history and the structured autobiography in situations where there has been little motivation for clients to falsify do believe that new investigations may be profitable. This is particularly pertinent when the documents are being used concurrently with other professional methodologies. The use of recording devices and communication by letters with a specialized structure and purpose is relatively new territory in some directions.

In short, with the normal, mature, self-actualizing client some psychologists are showing interest in considering communication as a process in which the interview is an important, but not the chief, dimension. In psychoevaluation this outlook appears to be particularly pointed and has an appealing face validity.

Brief mention is made of the need to study nonverbal communication as a possible major dimension when the interview is chosen as the communication vehicle. There are tantalizing cues regarding the importance of the interview surround: light, placement of furniture, and decor. We know little if anything about the possible differences between an interview held in surround A and a reasonable facsimile of the interview in surround B. Facial expressions, bodily tensions, physical movement away from, or toward, the client by the psychologist have effects not well known or understood. Psychological movement—with or against—is frequently reported by clients and patients even when the professional interviewer is unaware of the client-perceived communication. Psychology does have the methodologies for such studies, and because nonverbal communication is overt behavior, the research difficulties should be no greater than those encountered in some routine animal subject experimentation in studying learning.

With these and other reservations in mind regarding such heavy loading on the interview as a synonym for client- or patient-psychologist communication, the writer chooses to consider communication the proper term for describing the exchange of ideas, percepts, constructs, and conceptions which have been the body of this book. The interview is important, but it is a vehicle of communication—not communication itself. There is a hope that by restudying other vehicles—personal documents, nonverbal communication, bibliocommunication, recording and transcribed recording—we may emerge with better insight and understanding of, and by, our clients.

SUMMARY

Professional psychology is still seeking answers to many questions in the realms of understanding the three dynamics, dealing with clients and patients, arriving at accepted positions of practice, and selecting and training better candidates for graduate schools and departments, as well as in the areas of assessment, diagnosis, evaluation, relationship, and communication. It is the hope of the author that the shifting of the scenes and shuffling of dimensions into different patterns in this book may be helpful in finding better answers to some of our questions.

BIBLIOGRAPHY

Adkins, Dorothy C. 1954. The simple structure of the American Psychological Association. *Amer. Psychol.*, **9**: 175–180.

Adler, Alfred. 1935. The fundamental views of Individual Psychology. *Int. J. Ind. Psychol.*, **1**: 5–8.

Allport, F. 1955. *Theories of perception and the concept of structure.* New York: Wiley.

Allport, G. W. 1937. *Personality: A psychological interpretation.* New York: Holt.

———. 1942. *The use of personal documents in psychological science.* New York: Soc. Sci. Research Council, Bulletin 49.

———. 1950. *The nature of personality.* Cambridge: Addison-Wesley.

———. 1955. *Becoming: Basic considerations for a psychology of personality.* New Haven: Yale.

———. 1958. Pre-review of R, May, E. Angel, and H. F. Ellensberg (Eds.), *Existence.* New York: Basic Books.

———. 1960. *Personality and social encounter.* Boston: Beacon Press.

———. 1961. *Pattern and growth in personality.* New York: Basic Books.

———, and Vernon, P. E. 1931. A test for personal values. *J. Abnorm. Soc. Psychol.,* **26:** 231–248.
Amsel, Abram. 1961. Review of O. H. Mowrer, *Learning theory and behavior. Contemp. Psychol.,* **VI:** 33ff.
Anderson, J. E. 1959. The use of time and energy. In Birren, J. E. (Ed.) *Handbook of aging and the individual.* Chicago: Univ. Chicago Press. 769–796.
Angyal, A. 1941. *Foundations for a science of personality.* New York: Commonwealth Fund.
Astin, A. W. 1961. The functional autonomy of psychotherapy. *Amer. Psychol.,* **16:** 75–77.
Atkinson, J. W. 1957. *The assessment of human motives.* Princeton, N.J.: Van Nostrand.
Ausubel, David P. 1961. Personality disorder is disease. *Amer. Psychol.,* **16:** 69–75.
Becker, H. S., and Strauss, A. L. 1956. Careers, personality and adult socialization. *Amer. J. Soc.,* **LXII:** 253–263.
Bingham, W. V. 1937. *Aptitudes and aptitude testing.* New York: Harper & Row.
———. 1946. Inequalities in adult capacity—from military data. *Science,* **104:** 147ff.
———, Moore, B. V., and Gustad, J. W. 1959. *How to interview.* New York: Harper & Row.
Birren, J. E. 1958. Why study aging? *Amer. Psychol.,* **13:** 292–296.
———. (Ed.) 1959. *Handbook of aging and the individual.* Chicago: Univ. Chicago Press.
Block, J., and Peterson, P. 1954. Q-sort item analyses of a number of Strong Vocational Inventory scales scored on an Air Force officer sample. Univ. Cal. Inst. Person. Assess. and Research *Bulletin No. 7730.*
Boring, E. G. 1962. *Psychologist at large.* New York: Basic Books.
Brayfield, A. H. 1950. *Readings in modern methods of counseling.* New York: Appleton-Century-Crofts.
———. 1961. Counseling psychology: some dilemmas in the Graduate School. *J. Counsel. Psychol.,* **8:** No. 1, 17–19.
Brown, R. 1958. *Words and things.* New York: Free Press of Glencoe.
Bruner, J. S., Goodnow, J. J., and Austin, G. A. 1956. *A Study of thinking.* New York: Wiley.
———. 1958. In Solomon, P. (Ed.) *Sensory deprivation.* Cambridge: Harvard.
Buhler, Charlotte. 1935. The curve of life as studied in biographies. *J. Appl. Psychol.,* **19:** 405–409.
Burgess, E. W. (Ed.) 1960. *Aging in Western societies.* Chicago: Univ. Chicago Press.

———. 1957. The older generation and the family. In Donahue, Wilma, and Tibbetts, C. (Eds.) *The new frontiers of aging.* Ann Arbor: Univ. Mich. Press.

Buros, O. K. 1960. *Fifth mental measurements yearbook.* Highland Park, N.J.: Gryphon Press.

Burt, Cyril. 1958. The inheritance of mental ability. *Amer. Psychol.,* **13:** 1–16.

Butler, John. 1954. In *The Kentucky symposium on learning.* New York: Wiley.

Cattell, R. B. 1950. *Personality: A systematic theoretical and factual study.* New York: McGraw-Hill.

———. 1957. *Personality and motivation structure and measurement.* New York: Harcourt, Brace & World.

Centers, Richard. 1948. Motivational aspects of occupational stratification. *J. Soc. Psychol.,* **28:** 187–217.

———. 1952. Job satisfaction at various occupational levels. In Kuhlen, R. G., and Thompson, G. G. (Eds.) *Psychological studies of human development.* New York: Appleton-Century-Crofts.

Clark, K. E. 1950. Differences in vocational interests of men in seven Navy rates. Technical report No. 4. Department of Psychology, University of Minnesota.

———. 1957. *America's psychologists.* Washington, D.C.: American Psychological Association.

Committee on Definition, Division of Counseling Psychology. 1956. Counseling psychology as a specialty. *Amer. Psychol.,* **11:** 282–285.

Cottle, W. C. 1950. A factorial study of the Multiphasic, Strong, Kuder and Bell inventories using a population of male adults. *Psychometrica,* **15:** 25–47.

———, and Downie, N. M. 1960. *Procedures and preparation for counseling.* Englewood Cliffs, N.J.: Prentice-Hall.

Crook, G. H., and Heinstein, M. 1958. *The older worker in industry.* Berkeley: Univ. Calif. Press. Institute of Industrial Relations.

Cumming, Elaine, and Henry, W. E. 1961. *Growing old.* New York: Basic Books.

Darley, J. G. 1941. *Clinical aspects and interpretation of the Strong Vocational Interest Blank.* New York: The Psychological Corporation.

———, and Hagenah, Theda. 1955. *Vocational interest measurement.* Minneapolis: Univ. Minn. Press.

Deutsch, Cynthia P. 1958. What price psychology? *Amer. Psychol.,* **13:** 645–652.

Division 5 Test Use Committee. 1958. Graduate training program in evaluation and measurement. *Amer. Psychol.,* **13:** 467–470.

Donahue, Wilma, and Tibbetts, C. (Eds.) 1957. *The new frontiers of aging.* Ann Arbor: Univ. Mich. Press.

Eckert, Ruth E., and Marshall, T. O. 1938. *When youth leave school.* New York: McGraw-Hill.

Edwards, A. L. 1953. *Edwards personal preference schedule.* New York: The Psychological Corporation.

English, Horace B., and English, Ava C. 1958. *A comprehensive dictionary of psychological and psychoanalytical terms.* New York: McKay.

Eysenck, H. J. 1953. *The structure of human personality.* London: Methuen.

Festinger, Leon. 1957. *A theory of cognitive dissonance.* New York: Harper & Row.

Fryer, D. 1931. *The measurement of interests.* New York: Holt.

Galton, Francis. 1911. *Inquiries into human faculty and its development.* New York: Dutton.

Ginzberg, E., Ginzberg, S. W., Axelrod, S., and Herma, J. L. 1951. *Occupational choice: an approach to a general theory.* New York: Columbia.

Goldstein, K. 1939. *The organism.* New York: American Book.

Gough, H. G. 1961. Review of Sigmund Koch (Ed.), *Psychology, Vol. III.* McGraw-Hill, 1959. *Contemp. Psychol.,* **VI:** 154ff.

Guilford, J. P. 1959. Three faces of intellect. *Amer. Psychol.,* **14:** 469–479.

———. 1959. *Personality.* New York: McGraw-Hill.

Hahn, M. E. 1955. Counseling psychology. *Amer. Psychol.,* **10:** 279–282.

———. 1962. Forgotten people. *Amer. Psychol.,* **17:** 700–705.

———, and Brayfield, A. H. 1945. *Occupational laboratory manual.* Chicago: Science Research Associates.

———, and MacLean, M. S. 1950. *General clinical counseling.* New York: McGraw-Hill.

———, and MacLean, M. S. 1955. *Counseling psychology.* New York: McGraw-Hill.

Hall, C. S., and Lindzey, G. 1957. *Theories of personality.* New York: Wiley.

Harlow, H. 1954. In *The Kentucky symposium on learning.* New York: Wiley.

———, and Woolsey, C. D. (Eds.) 1958. *Biological and biochemical bases of behavior.* Madison, Wis.: Univ. Wis. Press.

Hathaway, Starke R. 1958. A study of human behavior: the clinical psychologist. *Amer. Psychol.,* **13:** 257–265.

Havighurst, R. J. 1957. The social competence of middle aged people. *Psychol. Monogr.,* **56:** 297–373.

———, and Albrecht, Ruth. 1953. *Older people.* New York: McKay.

Hayakawa, S. I. 1943. *Language in action.* New York: Harcourt, Brace & World.

Hebb, D. O. 1949. *Organization of behavior.* New York: Wiley.

———. 1958. *A textbook of psychology.* Philadelphia: Saunders.

———. 1958*a.* The motivating effects of enteroceptive stimulation. *Amer. Psychol.,* **13:** 109–112.

———. 1958*b*. Central stimulation and other new approaches to motivation and reward. *Amer. Psychol.*, **13**: 100–108.

———. 1958*c*. Alice in Wonderland, or, psychology among the biological sciences. In Harlow, H., and Woolsey, C. D. (Eds.) *Biological and biochemical bases of behavior.* Madison, Wis.: Univ. Wis. Press. 451–467.

Hilgard, E. R. 1956. *Theories of learning.* New York: Appleton-Century-Crofts.

Holland, John. 1962. *The Vocational Preference Inventory. Psychol. Monogr.*, Washington, D.C.: American Psychological Association.

Hoppock, R. 1935. *Job satisfaction.* New York: Harper.

Horney, Karen. 1945. *Our inner conflicts.* New York: Norton.

Huber, J. T. 1961. *Report writing in psychology and psychiatry.* New York: Harper & Row.

Hull, C. L. 1928. *Aptitude testing.* New York: Harcourt, Brace & World.

Humphreys, L. G. 1962. The organization of human abilities. *Amer. Psychol.*, **17**: 475–483.

Huxley, J. 1960. The emergence of Darwinism. In Tax, S. (Ed.) *Evolution after Darwin.* Vol. I. *The evolution of life.* Chicago: Univ. Chicago Press. 1–21.

Jones, H. E. 1958. Consistency and change in early maturity. *Internat. J. Human Development.*, **1**: 43–51.

Kahn, R. L., and Cannell, C. F. 1957. *The dynamics of interviewing.* New York: Wiley.

Kaplan, Max, 1960. The uses of leisure. In Tibbetts, Clark (Ed.) *Handbook of social gerontology.* Chicago: Univ. Chicago Press. 407–447.

Katzell, R. A., and Thompson, A. S. 1958. Some comments on "After Legislation." *Amer. Psychol.*, **13**: 652–654.

Kelley, N. H., Sanford, F., and Clark, K. E. 1961. The meaning of the ABEPP diploma. *Amer. Psychol.*, **16**: 132–142.

Kelly, E. L., and Fiske, D. W. 1950. The prediction of success in the V. A. training program in clinical psychology. *Amer. Psychol.*, **5**: 395–406.

Koch, Sigmund. (Ed.) 1959. Psychology: A study of a science. Study I. Conceptual and systematic. Vol. III. *Formulations of the person and the social context.* New York: McGraw-Hill.

Korzybski, A. 1951. In Blake, R. R., and Ramsey, G. V. (Eds.) *Perception: an approach to personality.* New York: Ronald. 170–205.

Kriedt, P. H. 1949. Vocational interests of psychologists. *J. Appl. Psychol.*, **33**: 482–488.

Kubie, L. S. 1956. Some unsolved problems of the scientific career. *Amer. Scien.*, **XLII**: 1, 3–32.

Kuhlen, R. G. 1959. Aging and life-adjustment. In Birren, J. E. (Ed.) *Handbook of aging and the individual.* Chicago: Univ. Chicago Press. 852–900.

Lecky, P. 1945. *Self-consistency.* New York: Island Press.

Lehman, H. D. 1953. *Age and achievement.* Princeton, N.J.: Princeton Press.

Lewin, K. 1935. *A dynamic theory of personality.* New York: McGraw-Hill.
———. 1936. *Principles of topological psychology.* New York: McGraw-Hill.
MacKinnon, D. W. 1962. The nature and nurture of creative talent. *Amer. Psychol.,* **17**: 484–495.
Maslow, A. H. 1954. *Motivation and personality.* New York: Harper & Row.
Meehl, P. E. 1954. *Clinical vs. statistical prediction.* Minneapolis: Univ. Minn. Press.
Menen, A. 1960. *Rome for ourselves.* New York: McGraw-Hill.
Miller, G. A., Galanter, E., and Pribram, K. H. 1960. *Plans and structure of behavior.* New York: Holt.
Morrison, A. V. 1961. *Individual differences in the ability to interpret gestures.* Unpublished Ph.D. thesis, University of California Library, Los Angeles.
Mowrer, O. H. 1950. *Learning theory and personality dynamics.* New York: Ronald.
———. 1960. *Learning theory and behavior.* New York: Wiley.
———. 1960*a*. *Learning theory and the symbolic processes.* New York: Wiley.
Murphy, Gardner. 1947. *Personality: A biosocial approach to origins and structure.* New York: Harper & Row.
———. 1958. *Human potentialities.* New York: Basic Books.
Murray, H. A. 1938. *Explorations in personality.* New York: Oxford.
Nosow, Sigmund, and Form, W. H. 1962. *Man, work, and society.* New York: Basic Books.
Office of Strategic Services Assessment Staff. 1948. *Assessment of men.* New York: Holt.
Olds, J. 1958. Adaptive functions of paleocortical and related structures. In Harlow, H., and Woolsey, C. D. (Eds.) *Biological and biochemical bases of behavior.* Madison, Wis.: Univ. Wis. Press. 237–262.
Pace, C. R. 1941. *They went to college.* Minneapolis: Univ. Minn. Press.
Paterson, D. G., and Darley, J. G. 1936. *Men, women and jobs.* Minneapolis: Univ. Minn. Press.
———, Gerken, C. D., and Hahn, M. E. 1953. *Minnesota occupational rating scales.* Minneapolis: Univ. Minn. Press.
Pepinsky, H. B. 1948, 1952. *The selection and use of diagnostic categories in clinical counseling.* Applied Psychol. Monog. No. 15. Stanford: Stanford Univ. Press.
———, and Pepinsky, P. N. 1954. *Counseling theory and practice.* New York: Ronald.
Pressey, S. L., and Kuhlen, R. G. 1957. *Psychological development through the life span.* New York: Harper & Row.
Riegal, K. F. 1959. *Personality theory and aging.* In Birren, J. E. (Ed.) *Handbook of aging and the individual.* Chicago: Univ. Chicago Press. 797–851.

Roe, Anne. 1956. *The psychology of occupations.* New York: Wiley.

Rogers, Carl A. 1942. *Counseling and psychotherapy.* New York: Houghton Mifflin.

———. 1951. *Client-centered therapy.* New York: Houghton Mifflin.

———. 1958. A process conception of psychotherapy. *Amer. Psychol.,* **13:** 142–149.

———. 1962. *On becoming a person.* New York: Houghton Mifflin.

Ruesch, J., and Bateson, G. 1951. *Communication: the social matrix of psychiatry.* New York: Grune & Stratton.

———, and Kees, W. 1960. *Nonverbal communication.* Berkeley, Cal.: Univ. Cal. Press.

Russell, R. W. 1958. Contemporary issues of concern to psychologists. *Amer. Psychol.,* **13:** 199–216.

Rychlak, J. F. 1959. Clinical psychology and the nature of evidence. *Amer. Psychol.,* **14:** 642–648.

Sarbin, T. R. 1954. Role theory. In Lindzey, G. (Ed.) *Handbook of social psychology.* Cambridge, Mass.: Addison-Wesley. 223–258.

———, and Anderson, H. C. 1942. A preliminary study of the relation of measured interest patterns and occupational dissatisfaction. *Educ. Psychol. Measmt.,* **2:** 23–36.

Seeman, Jules. 1959. Towards a concept of personality integration. *Amer. Psychol.,* **14:** 633–637.

Skinner, B. F. 1953. *Science and human behavior.* New York: Macmillan.

Smith, M. B. 1959. Research strategies toward a conception of positive mental health. *Amer. Psychol.,* **14:** 673–681.

Smith, Madorah E. 1952. The application of some measures of language behavior and tension to the letters written by a woman at each decade of her life from 49 to 89 years of age. *J. Gen. Psychol.,* **57:** 289–295.

Snygg, D. 1954. In *The Kentucky Symposium on learning.* New York: Wiley.

Solley, C. M., and Murphy, G. 1960. *Development of the perceptual world.* New York: Basic Books.

Solomon, P. et al. (Eds.) 1958. *Sensory deprivation.* Cambridge, Mass.: Harvard.

Spearman, C. 1937. *Abilities of man.* New York: Macmillan.

Stagner, Ross. 1961. *Psychology of personality.* New York: McGraw-Hill.

Stein, M. R., Vidich, J., and White, D. M. 1960. *Identity and anxiety.* New York: Free Press of Glencoe.

Stewart, Naomi. 1947. AGCT scores of Army personnel grouped by occupation. *Occupations,* **26:** 5–41.

Stone, C. H. 1948. Are vocational orientation courses worth their salt? *Educ. Psychol. Measmt.,* **2:** 161–182.

Strauss, Anselm. 1959. *Mirrors and Masks.* New York: Free Press of Glencoe.

Strong, E. K. 1943. *Vocational interests of men and women.* Stanford: Stanford Univ. Press.

———. 1951. Interest scores while in college of occupations engaged in 20 years later. *Educ. Psychol. Measmt.,* **11:** 335–348.

———. 1958. Satisfactions and interests. *Amer. Psychol.,* **13:** 449–456.

———, and Tucker, A. C. 1952. The use of vocational interest scales in planning a medical career. *Psychol. Monogr.* 66, No. 9.

Sullivan, H. S. 1947. *Conceptions of modern psychiatry.* Washington, D.C.: William Alanson White Psychiatric Foundation.

———. 1953. *The interpersonal theory of psychiatry.* New York: Norton.

———. 1954. *The psychiatric interview.* New York: Norton.

Super, D. E. 1940. *Avocational interest patterns.* New York: Harper & Row.

———. 1949. *Appraising vocational fitness.* New York: Harper & Row.

———. 1957. *The psychology of careers.* New York: Harper & Row.

———, and Crites, J. 1962. *Appraising vocational fitness* (revised). New York: Harper & Row.

Symonds, P. 1931. *Diagnosing personality and conduct.* New York: Appleton-Century-Crofts.

Szasz, T. S. 1961. The uses of naming and the origin of the myth of mental illness. *Amer. Psychol.,* **16:** 59–66.

Taft, Jesse. 1936. Translation of *Will therapy* by Otto Rank. New York: Knopf.

Terman, L. M. 1926. Mental and physical traits of a thousand gifted children. *Genetic studies of genius.* Vol. I. Stanford: Stanford Univ. Press.

———, and Oden, Melita H. 1947. The gifted child grows up. *Genetic studies Genetic studies of genius.* Vol. I. Stanford: Stanford Univ. Press.

———, and Oden, Melita H. 1959. The gifted group at mid-life. *Genetic studies of genius.* Vol. V. Stanford: Stanford Univ. Press.

Thorndike, R. L., and Hagen, E. 1955. *Measurement and evaluation in psychology and education.* New York: Wiley.

———, and Hagen, E. 1959. *10,000 careers.* New York: Wiley.

Thorne, F. 1950. *Principles of personality counseling.* Brandon, Vt.: J. Clin. Psychol. Press.

Thurstone, L. L. 1935. *The vectors of the mind.* Chicago: Univ. Chicago Press.

———, and Thurstone, Thelma G. 1941. *Chicago tests of primary mental abilities.* Chicago: Science Research Ass.

———. 1958. *Primary mental abilities* (second impression).

Tibbetts, C. (Ed.) 1960. *Handbook of social gerontology.* Chicago: Univ. Chicago Press.

U.S. Bureau of Employment Security, Dept. of Labor. 1956. *Estimates of worker trait requirements for 4000 jobs as defined in the Dictionary of Occupational Titles.* Washington: U.S. Government Printing Office.

Van de Castle, R. L., and Eichhorn, O. J. 1961. Length of graduate training for experimental and clinical psychologists. *Amer. Psychol.*, **16:** 178–180.

White, R. W. 1952. When prophecy fails. *Amer. Psychol.*, **13:** 656–657.

Williamson, E. G. 1939. *How to counsel students.* New York: McGraw-Hill.

———. 1961. *Student personnel services in colleges and universities.* New York: McGraw-Hill.

Wood, Ben. 1938. *The Pennsylvania studies.* American Council on Education.

Wolfle, Dael. 1954. *America's resources of specialized talent.* New York: Harper & Row.

Young, P. T. 1961. *Motivation and emotion.* New York: Wiley.

Name Index

Subject Index